MW00534122

THE VATICAN CODE

AMERICAN DIPLOMACY IN THE TIME OF FRANCIS

AMBASSADOR KENNETH HACKETT

Paulist Press
New York / Mahwah, NJ

Photo/Image Credits: see page vii for permissions and acknowledgments.

Jacket image credit: *Blessing of the Waves Flags Flying,* photograph by Jeffrey Bruno. Used with permission, jeffreybruno.com.
Jacket design by Sharyn Banks
Book design by Lynn Else

Copyright © 2022 by Kenneth Francis Hackett

All rights reserved. No part of this publication may be reproduced, stored in a retrieval system, or transmitted in any form or by any means, electronic, mechanical, photocopying, recording, scanning, or otherwise, without either the prior written permission of the Publisher, or authorization through payment of the appropriate per-copy fee to the Copyright Clearance Center, Inc., www.copyright.com. Requests to the Publisher for permission should be addressed to the Permissions Department, Paulist Press, permissions@paulistpress.com.

Library of Congress Cataloging-in-Publication Data
Names: Hackett, Ken, 1947– author.
Title: The Vatican code : American diplomacy in the time of Francis / Ambassador Kenneth Hackett.
Other titles: American diplomacy in the time of Francis
Description: New York / Mahwah, New Jersey : Paulist Press, [2022] | Includes bibliographical references and index. | Summary: "Inside the Vatican recounts the unique experience of being the U.S. Ambassador to the Holy See during the time of Pope Francis"— Provided by publisher.
Identifiers: LCCN 2022000063 (print) | LCCN 2022000064 (ebook) | ISBN 9780809106714 (hardcover) | ISBN 9780809187775 (ebook)
Subjects: LCSH: Catholic Church—Foreign relations—United States. | United States—Foreign relations—Catholic Church. | United States—Foreign relations—2009–2017. | Francis, Pope, 1936- | Hackett, Ken, 1947- | Diplomats—United States—Biography.
Classification: LCC BX1406.3 .H34 2022 (print) | LCC BX1406.3 (ebook) | DDC 327.456/34073—dc23/eng/20220304
LC record available at https://lccn.loc.gov/2022000063
LC ebook record available at https://lccn.loc.gov/2022000064

ISBN 978-0-8091-0671-4 (hardcover)
ISBN 978-0-8091-8777-5 (e-book)

Published by Paulist Press
997 Macarthur Boulevard
Mahwah, New Jersey 07430
www.paulistpress.com

Printed and bound in Colombia
www.milibroimpreso.com

CONTENTS

Photographs may be found on pages 87 to 90.

LIST OF ILLUSTRATIONS

FOREWORD

THE LIFE OF A DIPLOMAT may sometimes be imagined as an endless round of tea and cakes. But at its heart, diplomacy is about problem resolution.

In its highest form, it explores solutions to the greatest problems confronting humanity. Poverty, hunger, the climate crisis, racial or religious discrimination, and armed conflicts are just some of the most dramatic challenges crying out for wise diplomacy.

Technological progress has offered opportunities for advancement in care, communication, and fulfillment that were scarcely imagined a few decades ago. We now have more means than ever before to tackle some of our world's most solemn challenges and integrate people across the globe.

Sadly, though, recent years have also highlighted the dangers of technology if unwisely applied. In many parts of the world, instead of greater social harmony and peace between nations, we see an increased tendency to isolation and increased tensions and intolerance. Mistrust in international agencies has risen; the sense of our bonds as a single human family appears to have weakened.

As I write this foreword in the early part of 2022, the world is still struggling to control the worst pandemic of my lifetime. Among the numerous horrors around us are the immense suffering in Syria and now the worst conflict in Europe since the end of the Second World War.

I am conscious of the risk of striking an overly dark note that might do disservice to the interesting and entertaining book that follows. Ken Hackett's excellent account of his time as American Ambassador to the Holy See provides an insightful snapshot of the diplomatic life and an explainer of some of the workings of the Vatican and its status as a "soft power" in world politics.

However, none of us serving in the Diplomatic Corps accredited to the Holy See are likely to lose sight of the bigger picture and the quintessential calling of the diplomat to try to make the world better. Certainly not the author of this book, who has spent a lifetime working to address issues of human dignity and survival across the globe.

Ken spent forty years working with Catholic Relief Services (CRS). An organization born out of the refugee crisis in the wake of the Second World War, CRS is an official agency of the Catholic Church in the United States and a global organization dedicated to protecting and advancing human life by directly assisting those in need and advocating solutions to injustice.

Prior to serving as Chief Executive of CRS for the nineteen years up to his retirement in 2012, Ken, at various times, directed its activities for regions such as Sub-Saharan Africa, the Philippines and the Pacific, and East Africa. In view of these credentials, it was no surprise in 2013 when Ken was selected by the administration of Barack Obama as the new ambassador.

Ken was appointed shortly after the election of Pope Francis, and he duly became a well-liked and highly effective member of the Diplomatic Corps. His memoir thus offers a fascinating perspective on the first years of a groundbreaking papacy and the new pope's reception internationally, particularly by Washington.

As a member of the Diplomatic Corps, he enjoyed a ringside view of the Holy See's own diplomatic efforts to fight for human rights and achieve a just, free, and peaceful world. Pope Francis has been tireless in his commitment to universally promote the individual and collective good for humanity. He has been a "listening and welcoming" pope, but one with a global voice and a global impact, dedicated to finding solutions for the poor, refugees, and victims of violence.

Without being weighed down by the baggage of "national interests," the Holy See is in a unique position globally to bridge ideological divides and bring together warring combatants. Pope Francis's efforts to improve life for ordinary people throughout the world can teach us all the value of remaining open and empathic to those with different beliefs, but that diplomacy should also have an unflinching moral basis.

It is the aim of many of us who enter public life, including the world of diplomacy, that we can make a difference and contribute to leaving the world a better place. Ken has certainly done that over the course of his career, including his years at the Holy See.

I hope that I have not fallen into the foreword-writer's trap of tainting my comments too deeply with the concerns of the here and now. Ken's book is a document that, hopefully, will continue to be read long after our present troubles will be healed.

Ambassador George F. Poulides
Dean of the Diplomatic Corps accredited to the Holy See

ACKNOWLEDGMENTS

MY APPOINTMENT AS United States ambassador to the Holy See started when I first set foot in Ghana in July 1968. From that point—in the Peace Corps and throughout forty years working with Catholic Relief Services—I traveled a long providential road where, on many occasions, I received a room, a rest stop, and a listening ear. I was often welcome for a meal and wise counsel from many. I remember, especially, the men and women religious, the parish priests, the bishops, and the dedicated laypeople who were working to bring betterment and the gospel to all they served. Most memorable were those who supported me when I started out in Ghana: Fr. Rudolf Krajic, SVD, whom I lived with on the Afram Plains, and the religious sisters at the hospital in Nkawkaw who took me in one frightening Christmas, in 1969, when I arrived with a terrible, almost debilitating earache.

So often, the priests, sisters, and Church workers were the ones who offered insight that no government worker had or even could obtain. For all their help, I am grateful.

I wish to acknowledge my colleagues who served in difficult places and times, in one crisis after the other, who gave me courage to persevere: Jacques Monteroy, who handled Somalia, Liberia, and Sierra Leone for CRS in the worst of times; Pat Johns, who ran the Stankovic camp in Macedonia, which grew from five thousand to forty thousand Kosovar refugees in a matter of weeks; Anne Bousquet, who today remains in Afghanistan running CRS programs as she did in so many other hotspots; my mentor, Msgr. Wilson Kaiser, the African regional director, who always faced adversity with an optimistic attitude ever centered on the individual; and Mike Wiest, who throughout my time at CRS was a sage and clear thinker at my elbow when confusion abounded.

This book is mostly dedicated to my wife, Joan. She was an ever-present source of encouragement and support. She was the rock that gave me strength, from the first Thanksgiving I spent away in Sarajevo during the war, to the times I dropped into Somalia as the fighting intensified. Even through the endless stream of receptions and dinners in Rome that were part of the job and that, while not her "métier," she handled superbly.

More recently, this book was the result of Michael Hill, who helped me through many spots where I found difficulty getting my thoughts on paper. My thanks also to Paul McMahon, my editor at Paulist Press, who made sense of my incomplete ideas and sentences, errors in grammar, as well as sentence structure.

Thank you all and many more who crossed my path and made my life better.

INTRODUCTION

ON DECEMBER 23, 2013, I took a call from Karen Donfried, senior director of European affairs at the White House, at my residence early in my tenure as the United States ambassador to the Vatican. She indicated that she was calling at the request of Denis McDonough, the White House chief of staff, someone whom I knew well.

The call made me sit up and take notice, since I did not know Karen and her importance in the White House. More surprising was what she said: President Obama had decided to visit with the pope on or about March 27 the following year. He would be coming from a meeting in Brussels, and his trip to Italy would focus solely on Francis. It was clear that this was going to be a monumental occasion, so I got to work as quickly as the season allowed.

Our first Christmas at the Vatican was packed with liturgical ceremonies that we did not want to miss. And, as everyone in the Vatican is busy around Christmas, it was only on December 28 that I was able to get an appointment to see Msgr. Peter Wells at the Secretariat of State to inform him of the president's visit and to gather his advice. Msgr. Wells is an American from Oklahoma who wore the strange title of assessore (councillor). Essentially, he was the deputy chief of staff for the substitute for general affairs in the First Section of the Secretariat of State. That is a long-winded explanation, but anyone who knew Peter knew he was the go-to person in the Secretariat of State.

The March date was not fixed. Msgr. Wells cautioned that we should be mindful of Lent and the liturgical events that might occupy the pope's schedule at that time of the year. He also mentioned that Queen Elizabeth and her husband were visiting around the same time. We needed to make sure the dates would not conflict, but by mid-February, we had settled on a meeting scheduled for March 27 between POTUS and the Holy Father.

By early January, the possibility of another visit, this one from the secretary of state, John Kerry, began to emerge. This visit soon came to fruition propelled in part by the secretary's religion advisor, Shaun Casey. Shaun called Tom Donilon of the Archdiocese of Boston— Secretary Kerry's constituency—to ask if Cardinal Sean O'Malley thought the secretary's visit would be opportune. Obviously, the secretary was hoping for a meeting with Pope Francis. Regrettably, this was not going to happen. The pope, as the head of a state, does not meet with government ministers, no matter how important they are.

The secretary arrived on January 14, 2014. It was raining cats and dogs at Ciampino airfield where we met his plane. Any time the president or the secretary of state arrives in a country, the ambassadors are expected to greet them at the airport. We were certainly busy doing just that in the first quarter of 2014. The following day, we held an extended meeting with Cardinal Pietro Parolin, the secretary of state (prime minister) for the Vatican, and Parolin's then-deputy, Archbishop Dominique Mamberti. Kerry was accompanied by Victoria Nuland, the assistant secretary for Europe, Shaun Casey, and Jonathan Finer, the secretary's chief of staff. The meeting went on for one hour and forty minutes. We covered the world.[1] This was their first meeting. Cardinal Parolin had just recently taken up his position, as was also true of Secretary Kerry. A good portion of the meeting focused on Middle East peace and was linked to the pope's forthcoming visit to Jordan, Palestine, and Israel in May 2014. But the Syria situation, the hoped-for Iran nuclear deal, conflicts in South Sudan, the Central African Republic, North Korea, and Cuba also filled the agenda.

The secretary of state was expected to return on March 25, for a meeting at my residence that would include Prime Minister Benjamin Netanyahu, Palestinian President Mahmoud Abbas (Abu Mazin), and King Abdullah II bin Al-Hussein of Jordan. The secretary wanted to use the gardens and the house as an opportunity for a quiet dialogue. The U.S. special envoy for Israel-Palestine negotiations, Martin Indyk, would most likely also attend.

The preparations for that meeting were something beyond my belief. Security in the neighborhood was raised significantly. We had multiple security cars stationed on the street, a sniper in the cupola of the residence, the street cleared and cleaned, and an increase in interior/exterior guards. Flags of the three nations were placed in the reception room by the fireplace. The staff were poised for a major event. My wife, Joan, and I had arranged to get a room at a local hotel. And then, it was called off at the last moment. We were informed that Prime Minister Netanyahu had a change of schedule.

In any event, the secretary of state was in town and ready as we were for the president's arrival. Surprisingly, he decided to leave for Amman on March 26 and intended to return for the president's visit with the pope the following day.

Planning and Choreography

As we planned the visit of President Obama, everything had to be negotiated between the protocol office at the Vatican and the White House advance teams with the embassy in the middle. Among the negotiated topics were the number of people and cameras that would be allowed in the Apostolic Palace. The question raised by the Vatican's protocol office was, "Why did we need so many?"—after all, it was supposed to be a "press pool." They also wanted to know which individuals were official members of the president's party. The Vatican wanted to keep it to less than ten; the White House, of course, wanted more. It turned out to be ten plus the translator, the doctor, and the fellow with the "suitcase."

Then there was the question of guns. The Vatican was very clear that there were to be "no guns inside Vatican City." Presidential security initially pushed back but eventually relented (at least none were visible).

Additionally, the White House wanted a side event for President Obama. We searched possible opportunities. The Community of Sant'Egidio, a Catholic lay organization based in Rome, pushed heavily in Rome and in Washington, hoping that the president could visit one of their sites for the homeless or immigrants. We were aware of the Vatican Secretariat of State's concern about Sant'Egidio deflecting the attention of the meeting with the Holy Father, and Sant'Egidio's penchant for basking in the glow of the Holy Father. Though there was an acceptance on our part that they did great things, there was also an element of politics at play here. They were cut out.

We tried the Missionaries of Charity, which ran a refuge for the homeless right on the corner of Vatican City. Even though my wife volunteered with them, they didn't want all the disruption in the lives of their clients. Due to security and time, a side trip to Assisi and a visit to an early-morning Station Mass where many Americans heard daily Mass during Lent were also eliminated. It ended up that we were unable to put together a suitable and appropriate side event for the president. But after all, visiting the Vatican itself, with its halls and chapels of renown had as much to offer as any exterior side trip.

Air Force One

The morning of the long-awaited meeting arrived. The afternoon before we had gone out to greet the president at Ciampino International Airport. The arrival of the president of the United States was a big thing. We stood in a line at the foot of the staircase of Air Force One. From what I recall, the greeting line was the Italian foreign minister, the base commander, the Italian secretary of protocol, John

Philips, the U.S. ambassador to Italy, me, and David Lane, who served as the third ambassador to the United Nations Agencies in Rome.

The president seemed refreshed and energetic, with nice affirming comments for all of us. After greeting the president on the tarmac, we traveled to Rome in a convoy of more than thirty vehicles. The arrival of President Obama occurred at just about rush hour and was a wonderful chance for Rome's population to applaud on the sidewalks unconcerned about the traffic delay. The news channels were following the event, and most onlookers lining the route expressed excitement to get a glimpse of President Obama.

The next day the meeting was on schedule. We gathered at Villa Taverna, the residence of the United States ambassador to Italy, which was much larger than our residence and a safer place for the president to stay.

From there, we set out in convoy through the town in what was planned as a twelve-minute drive. The president's vehicle was tagged "the Beast." Of course, all the crossroads had been blocked for the journey, and my vehicle followed a security vehicle behind the presidential limo. That vehicle held armed and masked security officers with the back of their vehicle opened. I remember thinking, *We negotiated no guns!* There was no problem until we crossed Ponte Vittorio Emanuele II and traveled down Via Conciliazione leading into Vatican City. Just as we closed in on the gate to St. Peter's Square, the vehicle with the heavy security veered off. I breathed a sigh of relief.

Once inside Vatican City, we entered the San Damaso Courtyard and arrived at the Apostolic Palace. We were met at the door by Archbishop Georg Gänswein, the prefect of the Papal Household, and a group of *gentiluomini*, the traditional courtiers or gentlemen of the Papal Court. After greetings, we paraded into the Apostolic Palace, passing the Swiss Guard standing at attention, and into the inner chambers.

Archbishop Gänswein checked on the pope, and the president was then escorted in without delay. I noticed a woman whom I had not seen before quickly move by me and enter with the president. I had not even thought about a translator/notetaker because I knew that most likely Msgr. Mark Miles of the apostolic household would be there. He was quite capable of translating the Italian/Spanish into English. However, at this early stage of my diplomatic appointment, I was unaware that it was necessary to have a notetaker present during meetings between the president and heads of state.

The president stayed with the Holy Father for fifty-two minutes, a significantly lengthy period. Most heads of state's visits with the pope do not last that long.

Outside, I tried to keep the conversation going with Archbishop Gänswein, Secretary Kerry, and others. Archbishop Gänswein invited us to a window for a panorama of St. Peter's Square, where we discussed the health of Pope Benedict XVI. Archbishop Gänswein noted that he, of course, knew of the pope's intentions to retire, that he was held to secrecy prior to the official announcement by Pope Benedict but was free to speak afterward. In fact, he had given a few interviews about Pope Benedict XVI since the retirement and told us that the pope is frail but continues to play his piano, read, and write.

I did notice that the then Deputy National Security Advisor Ben Rhodes was particularly quiet and unengaged in our small talk. I was unaware beforehand that Cuba was most probably a significant focus of the president's discussion with the pope and that Ben Rhodes was a critical actor in this process of changing the relations between our two countries. He was obviously nervous as he hoped for a favorable outcome from the secret discussions as to how to heal the rift with Cuba.[2]

The doors opened and we all filed in for the photo shots and the presentation of the gifts. The president and the pope were both smiling and seemingly enjoying each other's company. I believe they struck a common cause around the Cuba deal and other geopolitical topics.

The Gift

It is expected that when a head of state visits the pope, gifts are exchanged. During a visit to Washington prior to the president's visit, a person from the State Department's protocol office asked to discuss the gift with me. She asked for my suggestions, but really, had already something in mind.

I cautioned that Pope Francis was not one to be flattered by something expensive. I suggested a historic letter or letters from Charles Carroll or other signatories of the Declaration of Independence or from Bishop John Carroll, the first Catholic bishop of the new republic, to the pontiff of the day. She rebutted, "How about a seed box?" We discussed this concept back and forth, and she seemed to have every reason why it could not be a historic letter but that a box of seeds from the first lady's garden would fit the bill.

My schedule was tight, so I suggested creating the box out of something historic and associated with the Catholic experience in the United States. From her office, I called someone I knew who oversaw the renovation of the Baltimore Basilica (the first Catholic basilica in the United States). He told me that indeed they had remnants of the original wood from the basilica's construction in the early 1800's by Benjamin H. Latrobe, who also designed the United States Capitol Building in Washington, D.C. I left the contact with her, and they had a box crafted from that wood.

The president offered the seed box for the papal gardens at Castel Gandolfo. Only a few months prior to the visit, Pope Francis opened the gardens to the public. The Holy Father offered a copy of his latest encyclical, *Evangelii Gaudium*, along with a medallion symbolizing peace. Pictures were taken and, after a few minutes, we filed out.

Meeting with Cardinal Parolin

The president, the secretary of state, the national security advisor, Susan Rice, and I then met with Cardinal Parolin, the Vatican secretary of state, and his deputy, Archbishop Mamberti. The issues covered were generally global, but questions of religious freedom were raised by Cardinal Parolin toward the end of the meeting. The president responded that he would try to find an accommodation with the

U.S. Catholic bishops. We concluded after a productive thirty-minute meeting. We said goodbye to Cardinal Parolin, and I left the president as they headed back to Villa Taverna, the large residence of the U.S. ambassador to Italy, and Secretary Kerry to his hotel.

The president met with the Italian president and prime minister. Then he requested some free time to visit the Coliseum. He arrived back at Villa Taverna around 6:30 p.m., where all the trilateral embassy staffs—the Holy See and the United States Embassy to Italy, plus the United States Mission to the UN Agencies in Rome—were gathered on the bocce courts in the rear of the Villa.

The president was relaxed and spoke to approximately six hundred assembled staff. He talked of his meeting with the Holy Father and commended the staff of the trilateral embassies. There was universal applause.

This was a major and successful visit and one that, we would learn later, had major geopolitical significance, at least in one important area, Cuba. Regrettably, the major success of the U.S.-Cuba improvement of relations blessed during the pope-POTUS meeting was to be overturned by President Trump six months into his administration. Interestingly, during the time of President Obama's visit, the entire Western Hemisphere was in a state of peaceful coexistence.

Reflections

People have been encouraging me for some time to write down my recollections of four decades with Catholic Relief Services (CRS). I had lived and worked in many countries with the Peace Corps briefly (1968–71) and for CRS thereafter. Eventually, CRS appointed me their chief executive and president. Following my retirement from CRS in 2012, I was appointed by President Obama to serve as the United States ambassador to the Holy See.

After almost four years as ambassador, the decibel level and frequency of encouragement to record my experiences has increased. My initial plan in retirement had been to complete the history of CRS started by Eileen Egan. She chronicled a large part of the organization's history from its beginning to about 1975 and the Vietnam War.[3] More recently, however, and with my wife's encouragement, I have decided to put down recollections of my time as ambassador during the pontificate of Pope Francis. I leave the matter of CRS history to a future work. I hope to offer an inside look at the role of the United States ambassador to the Holy See and a glimpse behind the curtain of the workings at the Vatican. It's a story that will interest those who have little understanding of the importance of the Holy See on the global stage, using its moral authority in times of conflict, distress, and confusion. Furthermore, this will be useful to future ambassadors or those who serve in the diplomatic service at the Holy See. Finally, for those many hundreds of thousands who knew me as the head of Catholic Relief Services, I want to share with them a taste of what I was doing in retirement.

Pope Francis has also made more than one reference to his possible retirement.[4] As he now enters the second half of his eighties, his time as pope has been nothing less than tireless. I had the unique position to witness a good portion of the first four years of his papacy. Recounting the stories behind the events and individuals I experienced and met during those four years means capturing the history as I now recall it.

I served as the tenth ambassador of the United States to the Holy See from August 2013 to January 2017. Four of my predecessors have written of their experiences in this most unique role. During my tenure, the lobby of our new embassy in Rome displayed the photos of all who served as ambassador before me. Beneath these photos, I displayed the books of Ambassadors Melady, Flynn, Nickelson, and Rooney. Each work shines a unique personal perspective on the U.S. Embassy to the Holy See, the workings of the Holy See itself, and our interactions.

The Holy See is the governing body of the Catholic Church located in the sovereign territory of the Vatican City State. (At times, the term *the Vatican* is used to refer to the Holy See.) The Holy See's diplomacy stretches back centuries. But a formal diplomatic relationship between the United States and the Holy See is a little over three and a half decades old.

Vatican City is not large in land area; in fact, Vatican City is the smallest state in Europe and in the world. It is a roughly triangular area of 0.17 square miles (0.44 sq km). The operating budget of Vatican City State is also small, running under $350 million, an amount about a third of the budget of Catholic Relief Services. Less than four hundred people are employed full time inside Vatican City.

Nevertheless, considering the reach of the governing body of the Catholic Church, the Holy See is worldwide, with approximately five thousand people working for the Holy See in about sixty-five different entities and with a budget that runs above $1.1 billion. This does not include the assets and property of local (arch)dioceses across the globe nor the value of the treasure held by the Holy See in Vatican City and elsewhere.

Given the sustaining worldwide presence of the Holy See through its embassies and emissaries, its perceived neutrality or non-partisan political positions, its disinterest in transactional diplomacy, and in many cases, its moral authority, it commands respect and is asked to play major roles in conflict resolution and peacebuilding.

Two recent articles, the first by Giancarlo Elia Valori in *Modern Diplomacy* and another by Victor Gaetan in *Foreign Affairs*,[5] address the Holy See's substance in two areas on the world stage. The first article begins with the statement, "Currently the Vatican is the largest and most effective mediator between the various ideological worlds and between the old, great political alliances." The second article outlines Pope Francis's approach to diplomacy in the Ukraine and the balancing of relations between the Russian Orthodox and Ukrainian Greek Catholic Church and other Orthodox churches.

The above-referenced articles touch on but two platforms of diplomacy. Vatican history is replete with many examples of diplomatic entreaties.

My story documents the many interactions on global issues and matters that brought U.S. foreign policy and that of the Holy See into alignment during my term as ambassador. I will also identify many of the actors and personnel, as well as those engaged around the edges, that influenced policy and agendas. I found that what led to success was the interest in personal interactions and human relationships.

During my first meeting with the British ambassador, he told me about Vatican diplomacy: "It's representational, not transactional." And I found that always to be the case.

The Holy See, as the center of the Catholic Church, is a powerful moral authority. Its global presence, its focus on human rights, protection of religious freedom, and the dignity of the individual gives it a unique and generally respected role around the world. It knows and witnesses much and it engages quietly and thoughtfully on a broad range of issues including geo-political, peace, human rights, and religious freedom. It was President Reagan who was quick to grasp the import of the Holy See on the world stage, particularly regarding the aggressive face of communism's global reach. He was the first to open official diplomatic relations.

My background of living and working for forty-five years with the Catholic Church and other groups around the world offered me a relatively unique perspective of the Church's social mission, and many of its intrepid and valiant personalities. Others can try to document and make the case for the global importance of the Church; I lived it.

This, however, is not a biography of Pope Francis; many have undertaken that task and can do it far better than me.[6] These reflections are just that, my reflections.

1

THE WHITE SMOKE

PEOPLE AROUND THE WORLD, even non-Christians, are excited when the white-colored smoke pours out of the Vatican chimney, signifying that the College of Cardinals has chosen a new pope.[1]

In March 2013, I had a personal reason to invest in the choice of the cardinals beyond the usual interest of a Boston Irish Catholic boy. I was being considered for the post of the ambassador of the United States to the Holy See. The first notion that the position of ambassador could even play a role in my life began with my decision to retire from Catholic Relief Services.

In 2009, I announced to my board that I wished to retire from Catholic Relief Services at the end of 2011. Having served forty years with the organization, virtually nineteen of which were as CEO, was incredibly fulfilling, and I was proud of my achievements and how they had impacted the lives of millions around the globe. But it was time that others should take up the mantle. I wanted the board to have ample time to pick my successor. Two years earlier I had asked the board for and was granted a sabbatical. But the economic recession hit us at CRS as severely as it hit many other organizations. We had to put into place a downsizing—early retirement buy-out options—to avoid a financial decline wherein we predicted that we would have had to cut back on mission operations. That was a less favorable alternative.

In that environment, there was no way I could accept a sabbatical. Painful as the downsizing was, the organization got through it. It was difficult to witness sixty-five folks, mostly friends, departing and carrying history and experience out the door. As 2008 passed, the economy began to improve, but after so many years without a break, I knew I had to consider retirement.

I had not thought much about what I wanted to do after my time at CRS. I was always one to play till the end of the game. Scouting options before leaving seemed disingenuous. Furthermore, I had always adhered to the attitude of "God will take care of it." There were only three occasions during my forty years with CRS that I ever really asked for anything. First, I asked for an assignment in the Philippines and Asia after an eleven-year stint in the New York headquarters working on sub-Saharan concerns. The second was to apply for the job as the CEO of the organization. The third was to ask the board of directors for a sabbatical, which they approved but I never took.

Immediately the announcement of my retirement plans, a bishop member of the board suggested that I consider the position of ambassador to the Holy See. I thought little of it. There were bigger agendas at play: the Haiti earthquake response; a decrease in U.S. government support for our large HIV/AIDS program; and keeping the attention focused on operations across the rest of the CRS world during those tough financial times.

Finally, in early February 2012, the day of the retirement party arrived. There were speeches, the alumni, invitees, the requisite kudos, some tears, and, as you would expect, some who were thinking, *Why did he wait so long?* and *What will happen to us next?*

Toward the end of my farewell speech, I noticed a tall individual, followed by a taller priest enter the back of the room. We gathered after the speeches to share best wishes and good cheer with CRS staff and friends from Baltimore. I was surprised indeed that Denis McDonough, the chief of staff at the White House, had bothered to come all the way from Washington, D.C. I had known Denis for some time, in fact, when he was a staffer for Senator Tom Daschle. I recall that he even traveled with CRS to visit Cuba. He indicated that he was pleased to be here and that he had just picked up his brother at BWI Marshall Airport. We toasted and carried on.

As folks were leaving, Denis asked if he could speak with me. First, he presented me with a letter from President Obama congratulating me on my service. Then he punctuated that gift with the statement that the president would like me to consider taking the position as ambassador at the Vatican. Even without consulting my wife—I knew she would not object—I indicated an affirmative response.

When we returned home, Joan and I thought that it would be an interesting and enjoyable post-CRS tour. But now, we really needed downtime. We had planned a "visit America" trip. We had lived across the globe and seen much of the world but not much of our own backyard. We toured the Grand Canyon and visited friends in Arizona. I gave a commencement address at the University of San Francisco and received the Laetare Award at the University of Notre Dame the next day. I was humbled to be counted in the company of such Catholic notables as John F. Kennedy, Dorothy Day, Walker Percy, Sr. Helen Prejean, and dozens of others.

Following the summer of travel and commencements, we returned to our small but comfortable condo in Florida, where we thought we might hear from the White House, but it was all quiet on that front. Although we had tried to rent the condo for some years, just as we had time to use it, a renter offered to take it for a year, starting in August. Off we went back to Baltimore for a cold winter.

Retirement was good but not busy. I continued to play squash most mornings with my regular group of gentlemen of a senior age. My son, Michael, was at Virginia Commonwealth University School of the Arts and my daughter, Jenny, was beginning her career in Baltimore. They were close and I was now a man of leisure, so we could enjoy and share family times. I started doing a little consulting with the University of Notre Dame as they launched a new project that became the precursor to the Keough School of Global Affairs.

Meanwhile, as is the case with most retirees, I was navigating the retirement world of senior discounts and Medicare. My cardiologist, Stephen Pollock at St. Joseph's Hospital, had indicated that I would have to have a surgery on my heart in the next couple of years due to a stenosis in the aortic valve. He counseled caution about any dizziness when exercising. Bob Oare, one of my squash partners, had arranged a game against two gentlemen from Columbia, Maryland, for a few days after Christmas 2012. I stepped on the court against a younger fellow who moved around the court much faster than me. Halfway through the game, I had to stop and sit down. The predicted dizziness had arrived.

I called for an appointment with Dr. Pollock. We had already planned a ski trip to British Columbia with the family in January; he advised that I should forgo the slopes and keep a close watch on how I felt.

It was shortly after we returned from Canada that I again felt dizzy, and Joan took me to the hospital where they scheduled surgery.

While I was hospitalized, Fr. J. Bryan Hehir called the house. He was a friend, my counselor at CRS, a chair at Harvard's Kennedy School, and head of various offices at the cardinal's office at the Archdiocese of Boston. He talked to Joan and asked to speak to me. She told him that I was in the hospital. He said, "Oh, never mind it's not that important." We later learned that he wanted to let me know that Senator Kerry had called Fr. Leahy, the president of Boston College, my alma mater. Kerry asked President Leahy to enquire with Cardinal O'Malley if he would have any objection to my nomination as ambassador to the Holy See. The White House would have raised the possibility of my appointment to be ambassador with Senator Kerry as chairman of the Senate Foreign Relations Committee. I do not know what Senator Kerry's relations with Cardinal Sean O'Malley might have been. Being a presidential candidate, an issue may have arisen since there were already differences with some other American Catholic bishops and the senator.

It was less than a week after I was discharged from the hospital that I answered a call from the Office of Presidential Personnel, asking if I would take a call from the office director, Colin McMann. He called the next day to inquire of my interest in the position of ambassador to the Holy See. It had taken a while from the first approach in 2012, but here it was. He indicated that I would hear shortly and more formally from the White House after he explained the bureaucratic and security process.

On March 13, Denis McDonough, the White House chief of staff, called to tell me that indeed the president intended to nominate me for the ambassadorial post. My recovery from heart surgery kicked up a notch.

We wondered what was the delay in how the decision unfolded. I do not know the answer, but it is easy to speculate possible explanations. First, Denis could have gotten ahead of others in the White House and there may have been other more viable candidates. It is after all, considered a kind of gift post to thank a political operative for engagement or support. I offered neither. I remained nonpartisan as CEO of Catholic Relief Services, and my financial support of the Obama campaign never exceeded $250. I was not a big donor, nor even what one might consider a medium-sized donor. I was not overtly partisan, although I was a registered Democrat. While I had met President Obama on a few occasions, I could not say we were in any way close.

The media was all over themselves with speculation as to who would be nominated. My name rarely appeared. Second, in early 2012, my predecessor Ambassador Miguel Diaz had not yet resigned. However, there were ample reasons to suggest that he intended to do so. The residence for the United States ambassador to the Holy See was not suitable for a large family whose children had to attend schools spread around the city. Furthermore, for anyone bothered by allergies, it also wasn't the healthiest of locations, sitting as it did over an ancient aqueduct on Gianicolo Hill. The residence also had to have radon gas amelioration. Finally, by February 2012, the election campaign was in full swing and was not the time to change ambassadors. Whatever the delay, I now knew I was now ambassador designate.

While awaiting confirmation, only a small circle of people officially knew of the appointment because government background checks had to be completed. I couldn't even explain to my friends and family why the FBI was asking questions about me.

We provided a list of individuals, family, friends, and neighbors, and the background investigators expanded the circle significantly.

Part of the background examination was to list every country visited over the last fifteen years, people whom I had met, and the topics discussed. This was totally unworkable for me; my life had been filled with international travel. I handed the investigator my old passports. If he wanted more specifics, I would be happy to answer to the extent that I could recall.

The financial review, while onerous, was familiar. I had filled out basically the same financial disclosure forms when I was asked to serve on the board of directors of the government's Millennium Challenge Corporation under President Bush.

"We Have a Pope"

I had been formally offered the ambassador's position by the administration of President Barack Obama in the first week of February 2013. The post had been vacant since late 2012. The current pope was Benedict XVI, an academic without a long history as either a parish priest or an administrator. He brought many gifts to the papacy and was certainly profound in his teaching documents. However, there was a swirl of events in the Church, from the sex abuse scandal in the United States to the turmoil in parts of the curia—the Vatican bureaucracy. Much of this was moving in directions that were difficult for him to control. He did not appear well supported by those in senior leadership positions at the Vatican; the cascade of events took their toll on him.

In early 2013, the Vatican appeared to be reeling. Benedict's personal butler had stolen confidential documents that were eventually published in the Italian media. Rumors and reports of nefarious financial dealings involving the Vatican were rife. There was even talk of a cabal of gay priests that held sway inside the Vatican walls. Internationally, the sex abuse scandal showed no signs of abating.[2]

Distanced from these rumblings of unsettling circumstances, my wife Joan and I thought the ambassadorship would be an engaging capstone to our long career of service to the Catholic Church through Catholic Relief Services. We had met when we both worked there and went on to serve all over the world with CRS, the official overseas humanitarian agency of the Catholic community in the United States. Suddenly, and shockingly, just a few weeks after I learned of my pending appointment, Benedict resigned. This just does not happen. Popes go out of office feet first. Benedict's resignation was the first time a pope had resigned since 1415. He said he was tired, but clearly there were many other matters weighing him down.

It was under these unusual circumstances that the conclave of cardinals had gathered in the Sistine Chapel beneath Michelangelo's frescos. And on March 13, after two days of deliberation, the white smoke told the world that they had made their decision. The citizens of Rome knew their part in the ritual, gathering by the tens of thousands at St. Peter's square, awaiting the first appearance of the new pope; the rest of the world watched on television. Who would show up at that window? Would this be the first non-European pope? Would he be from the Southern Hemisphere, where the Catholic Church was growing rather than retreating? Then Cardinal Jean-Louis Tauran, who served as protodeacon with responsibility to announce the decision of the conclave, entered the balcony above the massive doors of St. Peter's Basilica and announced, *Habemus papam* (We have a pope).

We got our answer when Archbishop Jorge Mario Bergoglio appeared. Being from Buenos Aires, Argentina, he ticked off two demographic boxes, but he was also of Italian heritage, so his election was almost a nod to the tradition that he was breaking. He was quite an unknown quantity as he did not come out of the Vatican curia, nor was he a highly visible player in international Catholic circles. At the age of seventy-six, many viewed him as a caretaker pope who would only lead the Church for a few years, with not enough time to put his imprint on it.

From a Catholic perspective, it was significant that he was a Jesuit, not only because he was the first Jesuit pope, but also because the Jesuits have a reputation as being open thinkers on issues such as relations with other faiths, their vow of poverty, and their vow of obedience to the pope. I had enough years of Jesuit education to know that order's intense independence was viewed by some as arrogance.

Jesuits are very intellectual, thoughtful scholars, but not afraid to act on their decisions.

So, I was not surprised when Cardinal Bergoglio announced he was taking the name Francis, for Francis Xavier was a companion of St. Ignatius and one of the Jesuits' most prominent missionaries. However, I was surprised when he said that he was taking the name not from Francis Xavier, but from Francis of Assisi, one of the most beloved saints of Catholicism, and of Christianity. The thirteenth-century reformer preached simplicity and poverty for Church leaders and is famed for his devotion to nature and the environment.

Pope Francis

Pope Francis certainly set out for his agenda a twenty-first century version of Francis of Assisi's admonitions. He shunned limousines and rode a bus with the other cardinals. He announced that he was going to live at the Casa Santa Marta guest house inside the Vatican walls, not in the grand apostolic palace. He asked to be taken over to Domus Paolo VI, a residence for bishops close to St. Peter's. There, he personally paid his hotel bill. The Gucci loafers on the feet of many Vatican officials suddenly seemed out of place.

Even more heartening was the story he told of choosing the name Francis. He said that "as things got dangerous" in the conclave voting, he was sitting next to his "great friend," Brazilian Cardinal Claudio Hummes, "who comforted me." And when he got the votes that elected him pope, he said that Cardinal Hummes "hugged me, kissed me, and said, 'Don't forget the poor.'"

Pope Francis said he took to heart the words of his friend and chose the name after St. Francis of Assisi because he was "the man of poverty, the man of peace, the man who loves and protects creation."

"I would like a Church that is poor and that is for the poor," the new pope said, counseling bishops to reach out to the poor, not to wait for the poor to come to them. He also encouraged those passing by the street poor, to look them in the eyes, at least dignifying them as people.

Qualifications

All of that made me think we were going to get along fine. After all, I had just spent almost four decades with one of the Catholic Church's most prominent agencies working with the poor. After I graduated from Boston College, I joined the Peace Corps in the West African nation of Ghana. I accepted an assignment in a very remote and isolated part of the country called the Afram Plains District.

I lived on a Catholic mission with a Czechoslovak priest. It was there that I discovered CRS. Honestly, CRS wasn't that helpful when we asked for assistance to finance our well-digging program in the arid Afram Plains. Interestingly, I still have their rejection letter following my first job application in 1971 framed, yet I persisted and ended up spending my working life going all over the world for this wonderful organization. I have seen how lives can be transformed when the words and ideas of the gospel are translated into concrete action for the poor.

That seemed to be what Francis had in mind when, just days after becoming pope, he visited a prison in Rome and washed the feet of inmates, including two women. And a few months later, he paid a surprise visit to the Italian island of Lampedusa. Located off the southern tip of Italy, it was landfall for thousands of migrants trying to cross the Mediterranean Sea, many from Africa, but more and more from the Middle East, escaping wars in Iraq and Syria. Tragically, it was too often landfall for migrant bodies as overloaded boats broke apart before completing the journey. Francis's actions were a reminder to the Christian world to heed the call of Jesus to "welcome the stranger," to treat these refugees with kindness and compassion.

Francis certainly had his detractors—those who thought he was anticapitalist and that by eschewing the regal trappings adopted by most of his predecessors he was demeaning the papacy. Such criticism only confirmed that this new pope was roiling the waters.

It was clear this was going to be a very different papacy from that of Benedict. One contrast was his popular appeal. On his July 2013 trip to the World Youth Day celebration in Brazil, upward of three million crowded onto Copacabana Beach to be in his presence and to hear the words of the first pope from their continent.

I had never personally met Archbishop Bergoglio, although I believe CRS sent some money to assist his Caritas in Buenos Aires in 2001 or 2002. But CRS board members who knew him attested that he was truly a bishop with the people. To me this was a pope with "dust on his sandals," and who was of the people, not of the bureaucracy.

Preparation and Approval

I was intrigued and began following meticulously his every appearance and news coverage in preparation for my new job. First, however, I had to be confirmed for the position by the Senate. That process was complicated. I don't think my profile fit the norm for political appointees. I contributed a negligent amount to the president's election campaign, had traveled to corners of the globe most Americans don't even know exist, had dropped into war zones, Marxist/Leninist countries, and conversed with some rather evil warlords. I knew the White House wanted to move the vetting along as there were Obama detractors criticizing him for not filling the then vacant position quickly enough. But I believe my candidacy may have challenged the background checkers.

In many ways, the FBI clearance was a rather passive process. There wasn't much we could offer other than suggest people for interviews, colleagues, family, friends, and neighbors. In the end, we discovered their meticulousness in pursuing their own leads and going much further than the names we gave.

We prepared throughout the spring, hoping to get to the Vatican by summer. We told our children what was in store but no one else. Joan and I started Italian classes and offered the reason: "we hope to travel." Then, finally around mid-June the public nomination announcement came from the White House. We were relieved to tell friends and family what was going on. We headed for ambassador school in Washington, D.C.

The U.S. Department of State's Foreign Service Institute's orientation for new ambassadors was a unique two-week experience. The campus is situated in Arlington, Virginia, across the Potomac from the main State Department building located at 2201 C Street.

Our class consisted of twelve ambassador designates and spouses. A third were career diplomats, some of whom had already held ambassadorial rank. This course was a requirement and, while it was "old hat" to a few, it was new for most of us.

We had presentations from virtually all offices at the State Department with topics ranging from the mundane to the profound. There was a distinct focus on management and human resource issues. It was easy to glean that this was the area that most likely burdened the headquarters administrators, and understandable for such a global organization.

All the lectures on the intelligence capabilities, the security issues (this was just a year after Benghazi), and diplomatic procedures were interesting, but Joan and I had the lingering sense that most would be irrelevant to our life at the Vatican.

The career diplomats who lectured, including David Pearce, a classmate and ambassador designate for Greece, offered wonderful perspectives. We, of course, had language training, which was fantastic and most professional. There were sessions on media training and how to handle the feared "ambush interview." How to handle the expenses at the residence was necessary, since entertaining is a daily, sometimes hourly function. It was important to separate personal from professional expenses, something made easier by our house manager, who had years of experience in apportioning our purchases.

But we took seriously the instructions on avoiding using government resources for personal use. I had seen abuse in many international organizations; it causes dissention among staff. Joan used the public bus system to get around town, and it was a rare occasion that she was in the vehicle when I was not present.

The final and quite memorable session was the "crash, bang, boom" class, or "one hundred ways they will try to kill you." Its realism was eye-opening and had an impact. I had traveled the world for forty years, into the most volatile spots during wars, revolutions, and turmoil, without bodyguards. But then, I represented only myself as an American—albeit the head of a large American agency. I was not an American ambassador—a significant difference.

Probably the most lasting memory was the focus of the ambassador as "boss." I had "plenipotentiary power"; in other words, my word was the last word. Happily, I did not have to oversee the operation of multiple security agencies, all vying to assert their agendas, nor other competing offices, from agriculture to commerce, culture, and so on. Mine was a simpler task. I only had seventeen staff, and the other offices of security, intelligence, consular affairs, etcetera were at our disposition, but I did not have to manage them. They came when I asked them to be available, and they were responsive and helpful.

All the ambassador designates in the class at the Foreign Service Institute had to receive Senate confirmation before commencing their new assignment. The course coincided with when we hoped the Senate confirmation hearing would take place. The summer was winding down and Congress would soon be in recess.

As the pope was traveling to Brazil for World Youth Day, Joan and I were hoping for and expecting a quick confirmation. The State Department's legislative liaison folks told us that it was highly unlikely we would get a confirmation hearing from the Senate Foreign Relations Committee until they returned from their recess in September. We had a renter in our Florida condo and a prospective renter ready to move into our Baltimore townhouse. A delay meant sitting around in a hotel room all of August and probably most of September before a hearing was even scheduled. This certainly diminished our enthusiasm for the new role.

I went to the legislative affairs offices and learned the names of the Republican and Democratic senators who were critical to the Foreign Relations Committee's scheduling of confirmation hearings. At the hotel, cognizant of the criticism of the vacant ambassadorship at the Vatican, I called bishops in the states of these senators. They agreed to make the necessary calls to their respective senators. Consequently, a subcommittee hearing was scheduled for July 30. While Pope Francis was speaking to millions at Copacabana Beach, I was going through what is called a "murder board."

To prepare for the confirmation, most ambassador designees probably went through voluminous briefings and reports. For me, Sheila Carey, the desk officer, shared what she knew, but she had never worked at the U.S. Embassy to the Holy See. I was also not offered extensive briefing papers on policy issues. I relied primarily on my own knowledge of how the Holy See works, what would be on top of their agendas, and the briefings that bishops and staff at the Bishop's Conference had offered.

There were few, if any, policy matters brought to my attention during the orientation. Nobody mentioned the pope's position on the Syria intervention, although it was imminent. On the Euromaidan revolution in Ukraine, there was not a peep. South Sudan, Israel-Palestine, China, Cuba, Russia; no one at the State Department's geographic bureaus seemed to make a connection with the Vatican nor the need to brief or consider the new ambassador's agenda.

To prepare for the actual Senate confirmation hearing, one sits in a room with about two dozen foreign service officers seated in front, to the sides, and behind. The questioning starts slow and easy but picks up pace quickly as they toss difficult questions that might be asked by the senators. It was an exhausting forty-five minutes, but I came away with a clearer sense of how to shape certain answers.

The next evening, my hearing began in front of the Senate Foreign Affairs Sub Committee. John Phillips, the ambassador designee to Italy, and Alexa Lange Wesner, the ambassador designee to Austria, were on the panel with me.

Who walked in to chair the hearing? My Boston College, class of '68 classmate, Ed Markey, the new senator from Massachusetts and the then chairman of the Senate Foreign Relations Committee, who had just been named to replace the new secretary of state, John Kerry.

So, of course, Senator Markey began the hearing by expressing pleasure at being able to confirm his college classmate as the ambassador of the United States to the Holy See. And then Senator Tim Kaine of Virginia, another Irish Catholic, talked about his experiences working with Jesuits for nine months, interrupting his Harvard Law education to volunteer at a vocational school in Honduras. He, too, was enthused about my appointment.

The "Francis factor" was clearly at work. The questions were easy pitches, and I slammed them out of the park. My colleagues at the table—John Philips and Alexa Wester—seemed surprised at how easily I got off in the questioning while they were grilled. The full Senate confirmed me on August 1 before they recessed, and we were on our way to Rome in September, before many thought we would even get a hearing. The white smoke had drifted our way.

2

THE VATICAN—
A GLOBAL ENTITY

HAVING SUCCEEDED IN HURDLING the confirmation process, Joan and I readied ourselves to leave for Rome. I divided my time during those hot and muggy days in Washington with meetings at the State Department, on Capitol Hill, with my predecessors, and with bishops of the United States Catholic Conference of Bishops.

The State Department meetings were not exactly what I had expected. As I mentioned, there was not a great deal of interest from the geographic bureaus whose focus appeared to be, as expected, on specific countries in the various regions of the world. Most of the geographic bureaus seemed, naturally, to look inward. However, the Vatican was a global entity. One notable exception was Julieta Valls Noyes, the deputy assistant secretary for the Europe and Eurasia Bureau. She had served at the Embassy to the Holy See as deputy chief of mission and chargé d'affaires from 2008 to 2011. She spent significant time briefing me on all things Vatican. She knew the issues and many of the actors.

Some of the functional bureaus that were focused on global issues were eager to talk. The newly created U.S. Department of

State's Office of Religion and Global Affairs was headed by Shaun Casey, a theologian who immediately became a strong ally. The Office of International Religious Freedom eventually filled in 2015 by Rabbi David Saperstein, was another supporter. The special envoy for the Holocaust, Ira Foreman, and the Bureau of Conflict Stabilization Operations both had specific objectives that wanted my attention and my interventions with the Vatican. There were specific requests from the office that dealt with the upcoming disability treaty at the United Nations to have the Vatican get behind some changes in the treaty. There was also a request from the new head of the U.S. Mission to the Organization for Security and Cooperation in Europe, based in Vienna, to convince the Holy See to change its posture at the European Parliament on LGBT rights.

Many in the State Department viewed the Vatican—if they thought of it at all—through the lens of the pontificate of Benedict, which was mostly about internal Church issues. Few understood or recalled the pontificates of John XXIII, Paul VI, or John Paul II, when massive changes, such as Vatican II, took place in the Church and in global politics, such as the collapse of the Soviet Union. The Department's view changed significantly as Pope Francis's popularity soared.

My meetings and discussions with four of my predecessors were much more informative than those of the bureaucracy. Ambassador Tom Melady (1989–93) remained active on international Church issues after his retirement. As such, he was helpful, albeit rusty on the personalities in the Vatican offices. Jim Nicholson (2001–5), the ever-active Republican operative and former National Republican Committee Chair, was fixated on the relocation of the embassy, which he characterized as an example of President Obama's disdain for the Catholic Church. This was important to learn, as we will see. Mary Ann Glendon, whom I had served with on the International Policy Committee of the U.S. Catholic Conference of Bishops, offered helpful guidance. Although she had not held the position of ambassador very long, from December 2007 until 2009, she had a good appreciation of how things worked in the curia from other assignments with committees within the Holy See. Of course, there was Miguel Diaz, who left in November 2012. He did not always have complimentary things to say about the State Department and how it administered things. He spoke of feeling trapped in a security bubble and that he felt his conversations in the house and his external movements were monitored. In fact, his movements, as were mine, were monitored and it did not surprise us if our conversations at home were also under surveillance. By whom, we could not say. We were living in an environment in which foreign, and maybe even domestic, entities wanted to track and listen to our conversations.

An example of this surveillance became clear about a year into our tenure. We were invited to an event at the American Academy in Rome, just across the street from our residence. My guards accompanied us to the event and then waited across the street at the residence, where there was a small room separate from the residence with a TV and chairs for relaxing. The event ended about 9 o'clock, and I realized I had left my phone at home. So, Joan and I walked back across the street. The next morning, the head of Diplomatic Security requested a meeting. He said, "Mr. Ambassador, you just can't leave your guards. We have you on camera crossing the street alone" or something similar. I apologized and asked that he not blame the guards.

In addition to the State Department meetings and those with some of my predecessors, I also went over to the White House to obtain any specific concerns or issues related to the Vatican. I met with Denis McDonough, the White House chief of staff. His sentiments were exactly as expected: "Any opportunity that comes your way to smooth the path with the U.S. Bishop's Conference should be pursued." We also hypothetically discussed a visit by the president to Pope Francis. He was quick to add, "When you think it is opportune, let me know."

Packing up furniture, arranging shipments, attending two weeks of language training at the Foreign Services Institute in Arlington, Virginia, and putting our townhouse near Baltimore on the market was occupying most of our time in August and the first weeks of September. However, a few other issues on the world scene inserted themselves into what, I knew, would soon be matters on my plate at the Vatican.

In 2012, President Obama drew a red line regarding the use of chemical weapons in Syria: use them again and the wrath of the United States' military would be unleashed. In August 2013, it became clear that the regime of President Bashir al-Assad continued to use chemical weapons in the form of chlorine gas against his detractors. The world held its breath awaiting a U.S. strike on Damascus. Ships were positioned in the Mediterranean ready for the order to launch missiles.

President Obama sought congressional approval to strike in August, but many forces prevailed against him. A Republican-led Congress was hesitant to support him on virtually anything, and the use of force in Syria in particular. Our allies the British, the Germans, the French, and others were equally reticent. Even President Putin wrote an op-ed in the *New York Times* calling the president to show restraint. Then, when I read of Pope Francis's call for a day of worldwide prayer and fasting on Saturday, September 7 against any U.S. military action in Syria, I knew interesting times lay ahead for me in Rome.

President Obama decided not to strike, but the pressure he exerted was enough to bring President Assad to the negotiating table, and within two years, he had given up a major part of his chemical weapons stockpile. However, sadly, he was still bombing and torturing his own people.

Our departure date was September 19, arriving in Rome the following day. Of the many times I had been to Rome airport, never had I experienced such a welcome of security, police, and a variety of embassy personnel to greet us. We had arrived.

Settling In

On reflection, I could have used that security escort when I first visited the residence of the U.S. Ambassador to the Holy See. That visit happened in the early '90s when then Ambassador Ray Flynn invited me to dinner. I was representing CRS at a Caritas Internationalis meeting, and since he had been mayor in Boston (my birthplace), we spoke the same dialect! I was told his residence was just up the street from where I was lodged in Trastevere. When I headed out to walk to the ambassador's residence, I went the wrong direction and ended up forty-five minutes late for dinner. My late arrival was most embarrassing.

I had been back at the residence again in February 2012, when I was asked by the White House to represent the president at the elevation of Archbishops Tim Dolan of New York and Ed O'Brien of Baltimore to the rank of cardinal. Miguel Diaz was ambassador and, along with his wife, Miriam, we made up the U.S. delegation to the event at St. Peter's Basilica.

Now the residence was ours for the next few years. Fenway, our blind Bichon Frise, smelled his way around, trying to figure out the lay of the house, the yard, and all the new folks he would meet there. He might have had some difficulty with the geography, but he needn't have worried about the people—they proved to be a wonderful team.

Roberto Andresciani, the house manager, was most welcoming, efficient, and in charge. Equally, the two maids, Magdalena Costache and Zophia Torba, were wonderfully accommodating. And then, running up the stairs from the kitchen, dressed as a proper chef was Sergio Ippilito, probably the best of his profession within the culinary staff of the Vatican diplomatic corps. He presented us with our first noon meal.

It was later, as I went walking in the garden, that I realized what having such a staff means; we were never to be alone. In addition to the gardener, I met a guard and learned that two would be present through the night, as well as two heavily armed Italian *esercito* (military police) stationed at all times outside the gate.

The life of an American ambassador and family was lived in a bubble of security and cautious communications. But generally, we knew what to expect.

As a side note, after the terrible Charlie Hebdo attack in Paris in January 2015, security outside my residence was increased. I went outside with the dog and the bodyguards one morning to find a female *esercito* carrying new automatic weaponry almost her own height. Italy, while not a high-risk posting, had suffered through the assassination of Aldo Moro, the former Italian prime minister, in May 1978. Ever since that moment, the Italian security service was upgraded and more vigilant. Similarly, after the assassination attempt on St. Pope John Paul II in 1981, the Vatican security apparatus was totally upgraded.

The residence itself was rented by the embassy from our neighbor, the prestigious American Academy in Rome, which was just across the street. Happily, I learned from a short informative brochure prepared by Suzanne Nicholson, the wife of one of my predecessors, that the house, known as Villa Richardson, was built in 1904. If not elegant, it was dignified and certainly functional with its master bedroom plus two additional bedrooms and a fourth in the tower where our son Michael used to lodge when he visited. Downstairs, there was a sizeable living room surrounded by windows overlooking the lawn and an adjoining reception room. These two rooms together could accommodate fifty to sixty guests. The dining room was small and could only accommodate ten or twelve tightly seated. We had a beautiful deck just above a most beautiful and spacious garden, where we held as many receptions as possible. We were to learn from an American archeologist resident at the Academy across the street that there was an aqueduct, probably built in the third century, that ran under the house and garden. This was most likely the cause of the mold in the subbasement, though we learned this condition was par for the course in most old residences in Rome.

The residence was conveniently located between Vatican City and the embassy, which was several miles away on the Aventine Hill. The embassy staff had prepared a prioritized list of about a hundred individuals that they felt I should meet. It was a good list, but it lacked some people I knew and wanted in my first tier of meetings, for example, the American cardinals who resided in Rome. Though I had met most of them in my CRS days, I did not want anyone to have the chance to say I ignored them. It was also a very useful way to learn the lay of the land.

I made a point of making early calls on Cardinals Burke, Harvey, Law, Levada, Stafford, and, shortly thereafter, O'Brien. He had just been made head of the Equestrian Order of the Holy Sepulcher, a vehicle to raise funds for the holy places in Jerusalem.

When I met Cardinal Jim Harvey, we recalled that during a visit to the Vatican with my CRS board chair, Archbishop Tim Dolan, that then Archbishop Harvey was head of the Papal Household. He had hosted a wonderful summer dinner for us in the garden at Castel Gandolfo, the pope's summer residence about fifteen miles south of Rome.

Cardinals Harvey and Levada had the most to offer in terms of advice on how to move about the curia. When I made a comment that I hoped I'd be able to call the sixty-five-year-old Cardinal Burke again for advice, I was stunned when he responded, "Well I don't know how long I'll be around." I soon learned that he did not consider himself in the best graces with Pope Francis and disagreed with several of his positions and approaches. This meeting foretold what I was to learn two years later concerning his very vocal opposition to the Francis papacy. A couple of years ago, a book was released by the Vatican correspondent of *La Croix International*, a French Catholic newspaper.[1] During the pope's plane trip to Mozambique, Mr. Seneze, the author, asked him what he thought of criticism from some American laypeople and clerics. The pope responded, "It is an honor when the Americans attack me." This became the substance of Seneze's book—attacks on the pope from wealthy conservative Catholics and some in the hierarchy. Cardinal Burke's comments in 2013 were a prelude of things to come. However, as detailed in Jimmy Burns's well-documented study of Jorge Bergoglio's time as a Jesuit provincial and then archbishop of Buenos Aires, Francis was able to handle detractors.[2]

This New Pope

Looming in the background of all conversations, of course, was this new pope. What were we all to make of him?

In August 2013, *La Civiltà Cattolica*, an authoritative Jesuit monthly, published an interview with Francis by its editor, Antonio Spadaro, SJ.[3] Here were my first substantive clues as to who Pope Francis really was. The pope's own responses proved most useful as a touchstone when reporting to the State Department. It served as an early profile of this new and dynamic personality on the world stage. Within the State Department, as mentioned, I sensed only marginal interest in the Holy See, but in the White House and many other offices, curiosity in this new pope piqued.

It did not take long to become an unabashed fan. Francis appeared to be the elixir that the Church needed to wash away the bad taste left by sexual abuse scandals, excessive clericalism, sour treatment of women, and the judgmentalism that was turning so many away from the Church. He was happy, human, and humble. One day, during those first few weeks—before I had met him at the formal presentation of my credentials—we drove into Vatican City through the gate next to the Casa Santa Marta, where the pope stays. The police stopped us as they had closed the entrance to the Casa because the pope's Ford Focus was driving up to the front door. He exited and saw a group of about a dozen young children in San Lorenzo soccer shirts, the Argentinian football club favored by Pope Francis. They were assembled about thirty yards away. He didn't just give them one of those stiff papal waves, he beckoned them to come over for a hug and photo.

My daughter and son, who were in the car with us, were beside themselves, as were Joan and I. It showed very visibly who this pope was, that everything we had read and heard about him was real. He was a pope of the people.

This was a prime example of what we saw to be the "new pope in town." He was not reserved; he was spontaneous. He was comfortable with people, not standoffish in any way—much to the anxiety of his handlers. There would be many more examples during my time when Pope Francis would break the mold of the regal pope.

The Head of State

From our arrival until the day scheduled for the presentation of my credentials to Pope Francis, I took every chance I could to meet those on the priority list and more. My decades with CRS proved beneficial. One of the first invitations I made turned out to be to Cardinal Laurent Monsengwo Pasinya of the Democratic Republic of Congo. Francis had convened a council of cardinals to advise him, the so-called C-8 (later C-9) group. Cardinal Monsengwo, the only C-8 representative from sub-Saharan Africa, was in Rome in advance of its first meeting.

We knew each other from many previous encounters in Kinshasa, and when he had come, on occasion, to the United States, Cardinal Monsengwo was a patriarch in the true sense of the word. From royal tribal lineage, he was regarded in his native land as a person of great integrity and held important positions in the final days of the dictator Mobutu Sese Seko's regime. He had been president of the Sovereign National Conference in 1991, president of the High Council of the Republic in 1992, and speaker of a transitional parliament in 1994.

He updated me as best he could on the expectations of this new group of cardinals advising the Holy Father. He made clear that the secretary of the group, Cardinal Oscar Rodriguez Maradiaga of Honduras, had bombarded him with so many requests and suggestions that Cardinal Laurent Monsengwo had arrived in Rome early to prepare for this first C-8 meeting. That's the only reason I was able to meet with him.[4]

Within the next three weeks I met several others of the C-8 group. Cardinal Valerian Gracias of Mumbai (Bombay) was most gracious and open to many different approaches, including consideration of women for certain senior positions in the curia or at nunciatures, for example, those at the United Nations in New York, Vienna, or Geneva.

Cardinal Giuseppe Bertello, whom I had first met in Kigali, Rwanda, before the genocide, had become the president of the Pontifical Commission for the Vatican City State and governor of Vatican City. The nunciature in Kigali was located on a street just below a military camp. During the 1994 genocide, mortars were fired and landed on his roof. He escaped in time.

Cardinal Reinhard Marx from Munich and Freising in Germany was most engaging. I recall a meeting at my residence when he sat on the couch between a bishop from Haiti, who spoke only French and

Creole, and an archbishop from Eritrea, who spoke Italian, English, Tigrinya, and probably some Arabic. Cardinal Marx moved with ease between Italian, English, and French.

In those early days, I also called on the ambassadors of major allies to the United States. One important piece of advice came from Britain's ambassador, Nigel Baker, regarding how one can learn from and influence members of the curia. He told me, "Ken, here at the Holy See it is not transactional, it's relational. You are not selling anything, and they are not buying, so if you want to generate good information and influence Vatican positions, work on developing good personal relationships."

A light bulb went off. This wasn't like other ambassadorial posts. There were no trade deals, no arms sales. We weren't haggling over visas or work permits. We were talking about influence, values, morality, and world leadership. Relationships would be the key. I passed that advice on to all the new ambassadors from other countries who would call on me when they first arrived in Rome.

It was striking to watch President Trump's first visit to meet Pope Francis in May 2017. I'm glad I didn't have to manage that one. Given the bureaucracy around the Obama visit and the desired "transactional" relationship White House staff wanted with the pope, I can only assume that those around President Trump expected even more deliverables during his visit to meet Pope Francis.

Ambassador as Convenor

One special role I quickly understood was that the American ambassador has tremendous convening power. In other words, if you send out the invitations, they will come. In my first week, I hosted a breakfast for three American friends, Fr. Mike Perry, OFM, the newly installed minister general of the Franciscans; Fr. Ken Gavin, assistant international director of Jesuit Refugee Services; and Br. Vin Pelletier, a Christian Brother whom I had known for more than thirty years, dating back to his time in Ethiopia. The three had never met each other, but at table, we discovered we had much in common as we traded insider reports from Syria, where the Franciscans and Jesuits both had people, to Africa, where we each had considerable experience.

This convening role continued during our years in Rome. Sometimes it was groups of old friends like Vin, Mike, and Ken, but within a few weeks of our arrival, we were hosting twenty people from the curial offices responsible for migrants, with representatives from various groups in Rome working on the issue of human trafficking. In the coming years, there were many such gatherings including those to meet special visitors such as the Homeland Security secretary, Jeh Johnson; United States Special Envoys for the Great Lakes Russ Feingold and Tom Perriello; Luis C. de Baca, the United States ambassador-at-large to Monitor and Combat Trafficking in Persons; Geoff Pyatt, the United States ambassador to the Ukraine; General Martin Dempsey, the then Joint Chief of Staff; many American university groups; and dozens more who had causes worthy of a platform. Many may consider the "hosting" part of the embassy's life as so much glitz and glamor. It can be that if you allow it to be, but on a deeper level, it sets the scene for ideas to flow. Certainly, gathering information is important, but such opportunities can capture the pulse of the range of the world's diplomats and others.

Sometimes it matched the needy with donors; those in difficult situations (e.g., disease, wars, and civil unrest) were introduced to problem solvers. It gave some with causes a chance to speak. It was rarely sumptuous dining, but more often a hub of connections.

On one occasion, we hosted a rather special reception for a delegation headed by John Podesta, who served as counselor to President Barack Obama and was responsible for coordinating the administration's climate policy and initiatives; California Congressman Xavier Beccera; and Katie Beirne Fallon, who served as the Obama White House director of legislative affairs. Podesta stayed with us and jogged in the park every morning; unlike me, he was without guards (although they may have been behind the trees).

Following the liturgy for the new saints, Pope John Paul II and Pope John XXIII, we held a reception at the residence, where we invited a delegation led by the head of Newsmax, Chris Ruddy. It included Newt Gingrich, Ray Flynn, one of my predecessors, and an expanded group of Republican talk show hosts and personages. I felt it important to invite Americans of all political stripes, which was captured in John Podesta's statement when I invited him to speak. He said that it was "miraculous to have all these people in the same room."

Shared Concern and Solidarity

Let me offer a few examples where we used our role and residence to introduce individuals on the front lines to those who rarely had the occasion to meet those who were in the vanguard. In his annual January address to the diplomatic corps, the pope called the community to engage on a multitude of critical issues.[5] For diplomats, the easiest and best way to do this is by finding the occasion to bring people together around issues or individuals. Here are some examples.

I have known Archbishop Menghesteab Tesfamariam, MCCI, since 2005, when my CRS board chair at the time, Bishop Bob Lynch, and I traveled to Asmara, Eritrea. We went to review CRS operations there. The political environment was not good. The Eritrean government was repressive and was putting pressure on the Catholic Church as well as the few foreign humanitarian organizations. The archbishop made no bones about the oppressive practices of keeping all young men, including his seminarians, in National Service and keeping them there for excessively long or even, at times, unlimited periods. Likewise, CRS was an American Catholic agency associated with the local church and was put under the same continuous pressure by the government.

I promised the archbishop that we would remain working in the country as long as possible but that the burden imposed by the government made things difficult. He understood the situation better than us.

Upon my arrival in Rome in 2013 and learning that the Eritrean archbishop was in town, I invited him to the residence for dinner. We had much to catch up on. He was about to issue a pastoral letter in May 2014 that could well have gotten him, or his priests, jailed or even assassinated.

That is when I first learned about one of his priests, Abba (Father) Mussie Zerai, who was in Rome helping refugees at that time, but who the archbishop felt should move to Germany because of Italian visa issues. I came to learn that Abba Mussie, a refugee himself, moved by the terrible ordeals of migrant journeys and the plight facing them in Europe, was one courageous and intrepid man. He regularly made himself available for refugees traveling through Libya across the Mediterranean. Not only was he personally passionate in his work for these people—most of them from Africa and many from his homeland—he was also inventive, creative, and persistent. There was no bluster about Abba Mussie. He was quiet and humble, but this demeanor could not hide his spine of steel. He was the real deal; his cellphone number, reportedly, is written on prison cells in Tripoli, Libya, and elsewhere. He got calls at all hours of the day and night asking for his intervention.

He set up an organization called Agencia Habeshia and had an article written about him in the *New Yorker*.[6] Despite such fame, his personality hadn't changed. He was humble and direct, and courageous in the face of critics.

He was there for those who try to cross the Mediterranean, those who look for a better life or flee from war or repression. Sure, he took heat. He really didn't care. After all, he, himself, was a refugee, and he appreciated what it means to be in that terrible situation.

I invited him and the archbishop to the residence whenever possible to give some individuals from the curia and members of the Diplomatic Corps exposure to these two courageous people. Most would never have had the opportunity to meet either of them or have such an insight into the plight of migrants. That opportunity was appreciated.

In 2015, Fr. Zerai was shortlisted as a possible recipient of the Nobel Peace Prize. They could not have found a better candidate.

Answering the pope's call to engage with those distressed and marginalized can be seen in how some women religious took up his concern for the migrant populations coming to Europe and the priorities of the United States government around the humanitarian situation. We were supportive of the efforts of the International Union of Superiors General (UISG) to send women religious to Sicily to assist the Church in becoming a welcoming venue for the migrants coming across the Mediterranean from Libya.

The Ebola epidemic struck Guinea, Liberia, and Sierra Leone in 2014 and 2015. The governmental public health structures in these three countries were overwhelmed. The Catholic health structures were also heavily stressed but proved to be islands of hope in what appeared a hopeless situation. There was an important conference call that brought together the operating partners from Caritas and Catholic Church on the front lines in Guinea, Liberia, and Sierra Leone with Vatican staff and ambassadors to enlighten and explain to them what was happening on the ground. At that time, we were pleased to have Tim Flanigan, MD, an experienced American physician who had just returned to Rome from a volunteer tour in Libera. He was helpful in interpreting the chilling information we were hearing on the teleconference. Such an event helped to rally support for the recovery efforts.

On another health-related event, the outbreak of the Zika virus, we put together a teleconference with the Brazilian ambassador. It included Vatican staff, Latin America ambassadors, and heads of religious communities based in Rome who ran medical establishments in Latin America. They participated in a presentation by Dr. Anne Schuchat, who was a top official at the Centers for Disease Control and Prevention, to offer everyone the latest thinking and status of the virus outbreak.

There were many more, and it is difficult to say if such efforts directly influenced Vatican policy. Regardless, they certainly took up the pope's charge, while also supporting the humanitarian efforts of the United States government.

3

MEETING
POPE FRANCIS

THE PAPAL HOUSEHOLD and the protocol office of the Secretariat of State chose October 21, 2013, for me to present my credentials to the Holy Father and meet with him briefly. Credentials are the official letters from President Obama appointing me as Ambassador Extraordinary and Plenipotentiary to the Holy See. This title allows the ambassador to represent the president with the sovereign state. Essentially, the ambassador is the primary and most significant representative of the president in the respective country, and her or his word is the last resort.

It was not long after my arrival that I found many attempting to accomplish "end runs" around the embassy to get directly into the Vatican. Happily, I cannot recall any such action initiated by the White House or the Department of State. There were one or two other agencies that wanted to cut us out because of what they termed the confidential nature of discussions. We nipped those in the bud. What we couldn't control was other American players.[1]

The date to present my credentials happened to be the anniversary of the canonization of the first Indigenous American saint, Kateri

Tekakwitha; my wife, Joan, suggested that a medallion commemorating that event would be an appropriate, simple, and suitable gift to the Holy Father.

Other ambassadors had indicated that this new pope was not keen on the protocol of kissing his ring, making big gushing demonstrations of devotion or lavish gifts. So, a medal of an Indigenous American saint might be the perfect gesture.

We immediately set about finding such a medal, but as October 21 approached, we couldn't find anything. We learned that many ambassadors brought expensive gifts, but the pope eschewed this practice. In the end, we came empty handed; he probably approved.

The credentialing ceremony was a major event. There was a "frac" suit—that most elegant of formal wear, often preferred in Europe—leftover in the embassy from one of the previous staff that I had tailored to fit me. Joan had a long formal dress and mantilla (or lace head veil). Our family had arrived, as had our friends. There were no early instructions as to how many would be allowed, so I invited as many as I thought could make it. Sadly, just before the event, Vatican protocol frowned on having clerics participate, so I had to disinvite Fr. Bill Joy, my high school classmate from Boston, Fr. Bill Headley, CSSp, a colleague at CRS, and Bishop Bob Lynch, a former chair of the CRS board of directors, all who had come to Rome at my invitation. This was painful for me.

We followed instructions given to us by the protocol office at the Vatican's Secretariat of State, the invited guests and office staff gathering at the residence. The *gentiluomini*—two gentlemen of the papal court, as they were titled—were to take us to the ceremony. I got in the Mercedes of the principal *gentiluomini*, Alessandro Felice, along with Msgr. Bettencourt, in charge of protocol; Joan followed with the other *gentiluomini*, Prospero Colonna. Our children and other guests trailed behind. Of course, my ever-present bodyguards were in a car in front, and two security cars followed up the rear until we entered the walls of Vatican City.

As it happened, all of this took place during one of the U.S. government shutdowns brought on by one of Washington's political stalemates. We had instructions from the State Department in Washington to curtail all receptions, parties, or manifestation of expenditure, either personal or business. This meant we were unable, as was the norm with every other incoming ambassador, to host a reception following the credentialing. This appeared odd to many other diplomats and the Vatican curial officials. To some, it was a downright snub. But most watched the news and understood what was going on in Washington. I found that a hand full of ambassadors and many in the curia understood or were aware of Washington politics and were sympathetic to our situation. However, such circumstances, I discovered later, were not duplicated in other countries. It was embarrassing.

We were dressed in our finest outfits. My son, Michael, the architect/athlete, struggled to fit into my tuxedo, which was much too tight for him. Jenny had purchased mantillas on Etsy that she handed out to all the women who were without them. Off we went on the four-minute drive down the Gianicolo Hill to Vatican City. We processed as a group into the Apostolic Palace, in front of the Swiss Guards standing at attention, with lances at their sides. When we came to the pope's office, Archbishop Georg Gänswein, the prefect of the papal household, who had welcomed us at the San Damaso court-yard, checked to see if the pope was ready. After a minute or so, I was escorted in alone, while the others waited outside.

As I greeted the Holy Father, the cameras were snapping from all angles. Being ushered into a room where the Holy Father is await-ing you is intimidating. Not because he is so esteemed, but more so because, as a Catholic, we believe him to be the Vicar of Christ and the head of the Church, which I had been part of and worked for most of my life. The photographers were ushered out, and with only a translator remaining, the two of us talked briefly about my pleasure in being given this opportunity to serve as the ambassador of the United States.

Some weeks earlier, I called upon Cardinal Giuseppe Bertello, the president of the Governorate of Vatican City State. We had known each other since the early '90s, when he served as the apostolic nuncio in Rwanda and then subsequently in Geneva. He was in Kigali when the genocide began. I had great respect for his noble efforts to close the fissures and ease the tensions that he clearly saw in that society before those terrible days in April 1994. When we met, I asked him what topic I should raise with the pope, and he suggested that I speak about the genocide, which I did. I believe he had a sense that Pope Francis, who had never been to Africa and was probably unfamiliar with the particulars of the Rwandan genocide, might appreciate knowing more. In fact, the Jesuits were significant in Rwanda in saving many lives, although he may not have met many of them.

Among my guests at the day of the presentation of credentials was a former longtime CRS colleague, David Piraino, and his wife, Nathalie. She is Rwandese and lost fifty-eight family members during the genocide.

My meeting with the Holy Father was only fifteen minutes; he was warm and looked directly into my eyes. He let me do most of the talking, but two of his comments in Italian stayed with me. The first, "Don't lose your sense of humor around here," which is good advice for anyone in any situation, and perhaps an explanation for how he keeps that smile on his face. And the second, "Watch out for the devil," which I found perplexing until I later came to understand that his "devil" is a ubiquitous evil that engages and influences many in positions of power.

My family and guests were then ushered in for the introductions and photos. I introduced David and Nathalie, and he gave her a special greeting. She teared up immediately. He warmly greeted all my party and then my office team. We then left Francis and were accompanied downstairs into St. Peter's Basilica, led by the Swiss Guards. It was quite an entrance. People were lined up behind the barriers at the entrance to the Basilica snapping pictures on their cell phones having no clue of this entourage.

Msgr. Francis Kelly, an American canon of St. Peter's, accompanied us around the Basilica, from Michelangelo's *Pieta* to the altars that held the tombs of Popes John Paul II and John XXIII, where we knelt to offer a prayer. These were very special moments.

We returned to the residence as a small family group and toasted with a glass of prosecco. The formal reception would be held later, somewhat anticlimactically.

But my time as ambassador wasn't all pomp and circumstance and celebration. Issues that would occupy my time as ambassador were brewing. Some back in Washington were trying to portray President Obama as disdainful of the Catholic Church. Provisions in the recently passed Affordable Care Act ("Obamacare") were seen as an infringement on religious freedom. Even the supposed delay in my appointment was brought up as evidence of Obama's anti-Catholic sentiments.

The Early Days

My first few months were more than a flurry of activity, from guests and friends visiting—I wanted to see them all—to priority visits and those whom I was meeting for the first time. My staff, a small cadre of career diplomats, was good, but they were emerging from their own storms. For one, they had been without an ambassador for almost a year. And they had been buffeted by the heavy winds of Wikileaks—the exposure of dozens of cables from our embassy back to the State Department that were released in 2010. The impact was still being felt three years later when we arrived. It was one of the many challenges dropped on my plate. By their very nature, confidential cables are often candid profiles of people and perspectives on topics of interest. They are certainly not meant to be public, and when they were exposed, it was damaging and troubling. There were people inside Vatican offices who felt burned. My staff encountered many curial staff who would not talk to them. From what I heard, many embassies around the world had similar challenges thanks to Wikileaks.

My approach was to face the reality of the leaked documents straight on and encourage my staff to be forthright. Our job was, in part, to collect information and to understand the positions of the host counties' interlocutors and their principals. That we profiled individuals in our cables was part of our job. That some in the curia didn't appreciate our profile was regrettable but not something we planned to change. However, we did become less specific in some of our characterizations of curial persons.

In my first year, my deputy was Mario Mesquita. Smart as a whip, he was one of those people with plenty of nervous energy who was either commenting on everything or attached to his phone. My personality is very different, so his street smarts and intelligence more than compensated for my shortfalls.

Mario and Kim Penland, the political officer, were often at odds, laying out the different sides of each issue. Together they gave me the information I needed to decide on actions or steps to be taken. Kim was assisted by a more junior officer, Marji Christian. Capable, intelligent, and talented, she proved immensely valuable on several fronts, such as negotiating financial agreements with the Vatican. Antoinette Hurtado was superb in public diplomacy. We had numerous events that placed our mark on the community and the Vatican staff.

That team of Foreign Service Officers, who rotate every few years, was assisted by Markus Bakermans from New Zealand. He'd been in Rome for years and knew the personalities and how things get done inside and around Vatican City. Evelyne McWade, who kept all systems running and on budget, was a godsend during the complicated process of renovating and moving into a new embassy building. Her Irish good humor and overall competence made it a pleasure working with her. Beatrice Mirelli, an Italian who handled protocol with grace, shared wisdom with a gentle hand. She opened doors as no one else. Uta Sievers, in public diplomacy, was a German national who had connections and experience; and Jelena Lazovic, an American married to an Italian police helicopter pilot, was so engaging and irrepressible that everybody took her phone calls.

In the early days, my time was seldom spent at the embassy but rather calling on Vatican officials, the various "mother houses" of religious communities, other ambassadors, and Catholic organizations that had their headquarters in Rome. I tried to document various viewpoints and perspectives of this variety of connections. The other objective was to open lasting channels of information and communication. I learned whom to invite to a dinner or presentation when we had a visitor who was a specialist on some part of Africa, Asia, or Ukraine, on nuclear issues, and so on. Such presentations showed that the embassy was open, inviting, and offering a positive lasting impression.

Relevant Agendas

In those early weeks, I was playing catch-up on the broad portfolio where Vatican and U.S. interests overlapped. One of the major issues was the upcoming Paris Climate Change meeting slated for fall 2015. You might not think this would be of much concern since the Vatican has a relatively small footprint, both geographically and environmentally. But there was a rumor that the Vatican was working on an encyclical—a papal letter sent to bishops around the world to be issued by the pope in advance of the meeting. Such a document would add significant moral weight to a more concerted effort by the world nations to combat deteriorating climate trends. In late 2013, everyone in the diplomatic community was trying to find out who had the principal portfolio for the early drafts. By early 2014, many signs pointed to Cardinal Peter Turkson and the Pontifical Council for Justice and Peace. This office deals with human rights, social justice, matters of war and peace such as nuclear nonproliferation, and a wide range of other items with very practical application. However, as far back as November 2010, the Pontifical Academy for Science held a symposium titled "Global Climate Change and Biodiversity," so it seemed as though their fingers were involved with the issue as well. As is often the case with such documents, the Vatican had it pretty buttoned up, so we never had the opportunity to offer specific expertise on the topic early in the process of its development. There were American scientists who participated in various aspects of the development of the encyclical, just not ones who might have been suggested by the Obama administration.

Of course, as Pope Francis strode rather dramatically onto the world stage in 2013, there were requests from various sections in the State Department asking us to prepare papal profiles and ferreting out likely views and actions on global social, political, and economic matters, as well as his potential appointments to important positions.

I later learned that as Pope Francis crept into the second year of his papacy and his popularity was gaining significance, many in the ranks of the State Department and the White House were looking with much greater attention at what he was doing. For example, at the worldwide ambassadors meeting held in Washington each year, the United States ambassador to Russia approached me and thanked me for our reporting on the Holy See. He commented that he read everything that I produce and that, often, such insights gave him strength of argument when he or his staff had to relate to or glean what the views of the Russian Orthodox Patriarch were.

At this time, there had been much written about Francis in English. Elisabetta Pique, an Argentinian journalist based in Rome, wrote a very personal portrait, as they had known each other in Buenos Aires.[2] The English edition was released in 2014.

Not surprisingly, given Francis's profile, books did start being published. This body of work helped me appreciate this man who was leading the Catholic Church in very exciting and different ways. Other works mentioned in the introduction helped fill out the profile of this new pope, with each adding a different and valuable perspective.

But I learned much more talking to people, to those who knew him in Argentina and to others who knew him when he came on his infrequent trips to the Vatican. For example, I had met an Argentinian Jesuit studying at the University of Notre Dame's Kellogg Institute. We played squash together during one of my trips to South Bend in 2012. In March 2013, as the conclave to select a new pope began, I wrote to him asking about the chance of Cardinal Bergoglio being elected pope. He replied, "I don't know his chances, but if he were elected, I would probably have to run away to Siberia." Fr. Bergoglio would probably have been his Jesuit provincial in the 1970s. His reaction might suggest the quote from the Gospel of Luke: "Truly I tell you, no prophet is accepted in the prophet's hometown" (Luke 4:24). As I learned later, the young Jesuit provincial had his difficulties managing his Jesuit confreres during the turbulent times in Argentina.

So, our profile began taking shape. The future pope was appointed provincial of the Argentinian Jesuit community when he was thirty-seven, quite young for that position. In this role, he led a community of men, young and old, who were highly educated, deeply committed to their faith, their principles of social justice, and their perspective on how the world should be ordered. These men were generally not hesitant to make their opinions known; indeed, they were ready to sacrifice themselves for their beliefs. In this role, Fr. Bergoglio had to learn to listen but then decide, developing a decisiveness he would bring to the papacy. Alongside this was an understanding that he may have, at times, acted a bit impetuously, a hard-learned truth about himself.

The future pope assumed this position during a very difficult period in Argentina. It is called the "dirty war." Thousands were tortured, assassinated, or simply disappeared due to their alleged associations with Marxist and antimilitary elements. Jesuits, particularly those who worked in the economically poorer communities, were steeped in these social justice orientations. There was a tension in the Jesuit community between the younger men who worked close to the poor and the older men who sought to appreciate the value of law and order and stability. The provincial was expected to mediate these two extremes represented by very passionate individuals. So, Francis had learned how to be courageous in decision-making.

We also learned that he was not always on the best of terms with the Jesuit leadership in Rome nor with some others in certain quarters of the Vatican. Consequently, he seldom spent time in Rome, and when he did visit, he rarely if ever stayed in the Jesuit curia though it's just a block from St. Peter's.

One of the American cardinals told me some years before about staying with Archbishop Bergoglio during a visit to Buenos Aires. One Sunday night, the archbishop told the cardinal that he would be going out for a pastoral visit. The cardinal piped in, "Oh, I'd love to go with you." The archbishop responded, "No, the subway is too dangerous at night." He did not own a car and used public transport to visit his parishioners.

There was a Fr. Jorge Bergoglio, the young Jesuit provincial; but there was then another more mature Archbishop Bergoglio. His foundations seemed to be cut maybe initially from some Peronist cloth, but his more mature views were sharpened and evolved as he spent more time with the poor. He was not trapped in an ideology, and he certainly would not succumb to using the Church for any self-interested ends.

The portrait emerged. What we had in Pope Francis was what many had seen emerge in the cardinal archbishop of Buenos Aires: a simple, humble pastor, who drew his strength from being with and among his people.

But it wasn't only the "people" who liked him. We learned that in 2007 at the Latin American meeting of bishops at Aparecida, a town near São Paulo, Brazil, Cardinal Bergoglio was elected by his brother bishops to chair the important committee charged with drafting the meeting's final document, showing the respect his fellow bishops had for his leadership. Furthermore, on the day he celebrated Mass in the Sanctuary of Aparecida, the people applauded at the end of his homily. No one remembered anything like that ever happening.[3]

By the fall of 2013, the world was realizing that Pope Francis was different, a man of the Church, who was probably not going to change doctrine or dogma, but whose preaching and pastoral approaches showed that he would apply that doctrine and dogma differently.

How Pope Francis quickly became a major player on the world stage was recognized by *Time* magazine when it named him Person of the Year on December 11, 2013. He had already received a similar accolade in the Italian *Vanity Fair* magazine the previous July. But the *Time* coverage had significantly greater cache.

About a month and a half earlier, Msgr. Peter Wells, an American serving in the Vatican's Secretariat of State with the unfathomable title of "assessor," called to let me know that he had heard from an unnamed cardinal that President Obama would be visiting in 2014. He wanted to know if I knew anything about such a visit. This happened about the same time that the Italian newspaper *Panorama* had reported that the U.S. National Security Agency (NSA) was eavesdropping on Vatican communications. It was amid our back-and-forth on this latter matter that Msgr. Wells raised the rumored presidential visit.

On the "bugging" issue, NSA took the almost unprecedented step of making a public statement, denying that it was listening to the Vatican's communications. So, I was able to assure Msgr. Wells that we were not bugging the Holy See.[4] The situation settled immediately, for the monsignor was able to explain the significance of NSA's public statement.

As for the visit, I called the White House's chief of staff, Denis McDonough, who told me only three people in the White House had ever talked about the idea and none ever communicated with any cardinal about it. Nothing was scheduled. But I encouraged the idea of a visit, using the call to plant the seed, even offering some insight into the pope's schedule, for example, when he would not be available.

Themes of the Papacy

As I studied this new pope in those early days, I became captivated by two themes of his papacy. The first theme is an underlying quality that has guided him throughout his priesthood and that he articulated, according to Andrea Tornielli, in his second homily as pope, and that is mercy.[5] Pope Francis even called attention to Cardinal Walter Kasper's book *Mercy*, stating, "That book did me a lot of good."[6]

The second theme has been his repeated exhortation for the Church, its members, particularly its leadership and others in lay leadership positions, to "go out to the peripheries"—to the poor and marginalized. Be present among the people, not stuck in an office surrounded by bureaucracy and bureaucrats. Not only did the pope call people to this challenge, but he also walked the walk in his own actions, where he traveled, in his appointments of new cardinals, and in individuals that he raised up. He well understood the symbolism of actions.

For example, as we have noted, one of the first trips the pope undertook was to the island of Lampedusa to give succor to the migrants crossing the Mediterranean. He also knew that after this visit he needed a person of deep missionary and pastoral leaning to represent him personally in such situations. As a wonderful example of that heart, he appointed an "almoner" to handle the pope's charity.

In a "back alley" in Vatican City, behind the grocery store, near the Santa Anna gate, close to where the Swiss Guards' headquarters are located, is the Office of Papal Charities (Elemosineria Apostolica). For many years that was the place to obtain a papal blessing for a marriage, a fiftieth wedding anniversary, confirmation, and so on. And indeed, there are some people in the office, unstuffing envelopes, taking the ten- to fifteen-dollar (Euro, yen, etc.) contribution sent for processing and postage. These same staff personally inscribe and seal the parchment blessing. One can visit and place a request in person or mail it. The sale is for the value of the paper and manuscript work, not the actual spiritual blessing.

The office handles the pope's personal charitable giving. History tells us that, for decades or even centuries, the popes' charities were basically financed by this minimal source of funding. They, of course, had access to other gifts, but this office ran a small and inactive operation.

Early during my tenure, I heard a tale that a Fr. Konrad Krajewski was staying at Casa Santa Marta, the new residence of Pope Francis. (He was close to Pope John Paul II—in fact, a pallbearer at his funeral). Apparently, he made a ritual of waiting until after dinner when most had left the dining hall. He then went around collecting the bread and other food items that were salvageable from the tables.

One night, in August 2013, the pope called him over and asked what he did with all the food he collected. Nervous and probably trembling, he told the Holy Father that he took it out to give to the many homeless in Rome.

I can only imagine that the pope told him to continue his good work. Then, a few days later, the pope called him and said, "Give up your desk; you are to be my almoner. I am going to make you a bishop, no, an archbishop." And thus, began Archbishop Krajewski's time as the almoner.

The pope dispatched him immediately to Lampedusa to see what could be done for the migrants coming across the Mediterranean to Italy in search of safety and a hopeful new life in Europe. Press reports wrote of their desperate conditions in the hands of traffickers.

Archbishop Krajewski, most probably after researching the issue among the homeless in Rome, carried with him what I considered a wonderful gift. He brought phone cards. Imagine having left Eritrea, South Sudan, or Mali, and then moving through the desert for months, maybe even being held prisoner in Libya or some other North African town. Now, finally in Italy, wouldn't a phone call to allay the fears of a wife or mother be the first thing needed upon arrival? The phone card and access to a cell phone was a brilliant idea, and a practical way to bring the Holy Father's concern to the peripheries.

Pope Francis has sought to increase the roles for women in the leadership of the Church. The embassy embraced and encouraged this approach.

The editors of the book *Women, Religion, and Peacebuilding* list over a dozen women religious who have gained some measure of public recognition for what they have contributed to the cause and conclusion of peace efforts.[7] They recognize, however, that there are much larger groups of women religious who practice a "strategic invisibility." They write,

> There are many women across the world and religious traditions, whose work for peace is motivated and shaped by their religious faith and beliefs. Most work without recognition. Despite their enormous challenges, women religious peacebuilders have found ways to build peace that have eluded others. One reason is that their very invisibility creates opportunities that others do not have.[8]

A superb example of this model is found in a project of the UISG (the International Union of Superiors Generals, a grouping of almost 1900 heads of communities of women religious) that the United States Embassy supported in Rome. It was a network called Talitha Kum (or the International Network of Consecrated Life against Trafficking in Persons).[9] This is an effort of the UISG in responding to human trafficking. The embassy gave them a few small grants to support their anti–human trafficking projects. Sr. Carmen Sammut, president of the International Union of Superiors General, who lived down the street from me on the Gianicolo Hill, noted, "Without awareness, without acting together in favor of human dignity, the World Cup finals may turn out to be a terrible shame instead of a feast for humanity."

Notably, they undertook a major effort to stymie and stop child prostitution, or more specifically, a shaming of those hitting on and soliciting women during the World Cup in Brazil 2014. They mounted a massive public relations campaign in Rio. The campaign organized by Sr. Estrella Castelone, FMA, was titled "Play for Life, Report Trafficking." It involved religious sisters and others handing out leaflets at airports and key tourist areas in Brazil, encouraging people to report any suspected child prostitution or enslavement to police.

This took courage, for the traffickers of these young victims play rough. Naming and shaming had to have some impact, and the effort brought to light a terrible curse associated with these sporting events. Exposing this evil culture reinforced the social justice concerns of Pope Francis. Very early in his pontificate, he identified the human trafficking as a serious societal ill.[10]

We attempted to raise up some of these unbelievably courageous efforts of women in the Church to demonstrate why women must play a more prominent role in Church leadership.

South Sudan

While I was working with Catholic Relief Services and attending meetings in Rome, I was asked to meet a group of men from different religious orders who wanted to discuss a proposal concerning South Sudan, certainly one of the peripheries. Catholic Relief Services had a long history of operations in South Sudan and an extensive presence there.

What was being proposed was a new and innovative undertaking. I was aware that the separate country of South Sudan was in the making. In the interim, these men foresaw the great need for trained individuals to shape and lead the future institutions in the new country. The proposal was to create a union of various men and women religious from different communities, nations, and with skills. They would focus and assist in the needs of the people, the Church, and the nation, pooling together people and financial resources.

The ingenuity of the approach was found in the intercommunity approach, which was anything but normative. The Comboni Missionaries, and many other Catholic religious/missionary groups, had their foothold in Sudan, whose history was "their" history. This approach called for collaboration—sharing resources and talents in a single vision. It required overlapping territory and techniques. I thought it was imaginative and innovative. I offered some advice about how it may proceed and observed the progress over the next few years

Sr. Cathy Arata, an American member of the School Sisters of Notre Dame, whose mother house was a block from my own house in Baltimore, eventually became a liaison with CRS after being posted to South Sudan. She became part of this effort, which became known as Solidarity with South Sudan.

In its formative years, the effort was adopted by the UISG based in Rome. As ambassador, I touched base with UISG and learned that Solidarity had more than two dozen religious men and woman working together in various locations in South Sudan. The main work of Solidarity, as written in their mission statement, continues to be capacity building at the Catholic Health Training Institute in Wau, Solidarity Teacher Training Center (STTC) in Yambio, the Sustainable Agricultural Project (SAP) in Riimenze, and pastoral programs out of Juba. The organization also had significant operations in Malakal until the violence in the town in 2014 basically left the town in ruins.

The challenges that they personally have experienced are outweighed by their accomplishments in bringing hope and spiritual nourishment to many thousands. The gifts of training have been transferred, but not without personal pain and trauma.

During my time as ambassador, I learned of Mother Marie-Josephine Gaudette, an American sister in Rome, who was celebrating 113 years. Joan and I visited and brought her a cake. Interestingly,

Sr. Yudith Periera Rico, one of the sisters who lived with her, had taken over as the assistant director of the Solidarity effort.

During 2014, the members of Solidarity were under intense pressure and had suffered greatly. Sr. Yudith was a rock of stability. In 2016, a friend and member of her community was assassinated in Haiti. They were close friends. This I thought would completely paralyze her, but no, she carried on working even harder in her commitment to the people of South Sudan.

The pope has repeatedly recognized their good work, particularly in his hopes to travel to South Sudan. These are the peripheries.

The First Synod

Pope Francis's focus on mercy is particularly appealing as a recognition that we are all fallible and that an appeal to God's mercy can relieve some of our pain and guilt.

Early in his papacy, the pope called for a global Synod on the Family.[11] This was a matter fraught with controversy. It was to take place in two sessions spaced a year apart. He invited and encouraged considerable input from the laity, although in some dioceses it was not implemented as an open process.

The first session was controversial as he refused to give specific thematic direction but allowed the bishops to struggle with an agenda. Controversy ensued. The Americans and Europeans were occupied with divorce, annulments, and gay marriage, while the Africans were trying to deal with the family in the community, polygamy and conversion, and migration; important issues in Latin America were raised as well. There were many different elements in this complex but fundamental matter.

In an interesting approach, Francis let them air rather freely in the first part of the synod. Aware of the controversial reality of the issue, before the second session he declared that he would hold Jubilee of Mercy at the close of the second session. This was a way to dissipate the rancor and vitriol generated by those who thought that he was too soft by embracing Catholics in troubled situations who wanted annulments and divorces. His call was for mercy.

Everything Pope Francis did: where he traveled, who he appointed as new bishops or cardinals, and how he prioritized issues, was tempered by an exhibition that God's mercy is always there if it is asked for.

The Pope's Agenda

Every year in early January, the pope addresses the diplomatic corps. It is a time when he comments on the events of the past year and looks forward to the year ahead, identifying priorities, issues of primary concern, and even travel plans.

At my first address in January 2014, we were ushered into the impressive Sala Regia Hall, where diplomats were seated facing each other, with family and staff seated behind. On the walls of the Sala Regia are beautiful murals that capture some of the historic and often tragic moments in the life of the Church from the sixteenth century, and from where you can enter the Sistine Chapel directly.

The pope spoke of a few things. First, he raised the importance of the "culture of encounter," engaging one another with respect, which is first learned in the family. He then spoke about the elderly and the unborn and those who suffer torment in the family. One could see that the family was on his mind and a major item on his agenda.

He proceeded to highlight geographic concerns, with Syria leading the list. He praised the welcoming by Jordan and Lebanon of millions of refugees while recognizing that their burden was huge.

He also mentioned his hope for an Iran nuclear deal by the P5+1,[12] which eventually generated an agreement that President Trump abandoned a few years later.

He announced his travel to Jordan, Israel, and Palestine, which indeed took place in 2014, where he stopped to pray at a wall that separates Israel from the West Bank in the city of Bethlehem. This was characterized as a symbolic, unprecedented, and seemingly spontaneous gesture. The Israeli ambassador said later that the Israeli authorities were initially caught off guard but recovered when he stopped to pray at the Yad Vashem memorial.

His travel, be it to South Korea, where he spoke in English for the first time of reconciliation between the North and South; to the European parliament in Strasbourg, where he asked the European nations to open their hearts generously to the refugee flows from sub-Saharan Africa and war-torn Syria, were generally focused on that culture of engagement with the poor, the alienated, and the marginalized. Other themes raised by the pope were peace, reconciliation, ecumenism, particularly with the Orthodox, and interfaith understanding with Islam.

His later trips to Sri Lanka and Bosnia Herzegovina, his second brief visit to Cuba, and his meeting with the Russian Patriarch Kirill followed this same agenda that he set during the meetings with the diplomatic corps.

Popes before St. Pope John Paul II rarely traveled outside the Vatican and Italy. Pope Francis appears to be setting a record-breaking pace, despite making some early remarks about not wishing to travel much. He has dipped broadly into sub-Saharan Africa and Latin America and to a lesser extent Asia. He has not given significant attention to Western or Eastern Europe.

Nevertheless, the symbolism of a papal visit remains important and is relished by most local churches and governments. At times, though, his comments cause some to hold their breath and look at their feet as he unleashes rebukes on governments that fail to be welcoming to refugees or who may be less than sensitive to religious freedoms and human rights.

4

A CHALLENGE OF THE CONCLAVE

AS NOTED EARLIER, shortly after Pope Francis became the pontiff, he established a group of eight cardinals. It was sometimes referred to as the C-8 (and later, the C-9). Notably absent from the group was Cardinal Bertone, the then secretary of state, which was no great surprise as it was expected that Francis would replace him as soon as he could. Initially, most of the C-9 members were not working within the Vatican—seeking counsel outside the curia was a clean break from the practice of past popes. It was also a sure sign that management was going to be different. Their role was to help him handle the many changes that he felt were needed in the Church, including the reform of the curia.

The assemblage of cardinals in the C-9 represented regional groups. Cardinal Laurent Monsengwo Pasinya of the Democratic Republic of Congo represented the church from sub-Saharan Africa and its convening body SECAM. Oswald Cardinal Gracias of India represented the church from Asia and its regional body, the Federation of Asian Bishops' Conferences (FABC). Cardinal Reinhard Marx stood at the helm of the European Council of Bishops and, of course, the powerful German church. Cardinal Francisco Javier Errazuriz Ossa of Chile, a former president of CELAM, represented the church from Latin America. Then there was Cardinal George Pell of Australia who, it might be claimed, lead the Federation of Catholic Bishops' Conferences of Oceania, Cardinal Sean O'Malley of Boston, and Cardinal Oscar Rodriguez Maradiaga of Honduras, who was designated by the pope as the chair. Added to this quasi-regional representation were cardinals that targeted other matters, including Cardinal Giuseppe Bertolo, president of the Vatican City State (the Governorate), and eventually, when he arrived in Rome to take up his position as secretary of state in late 2013, Cardinal Pietro Parolin.

The pope convened this group on an almost quarterly basis. Their charge is to advise and help the pope govern the universal Church, a broad mandate. Reflecting on my time at the embassy, this group covered a large number of substantive matters. The diverse problems of family and marriage, ranging from divorced Catholics to polygamist converts and many cultural obstacles in between, required this worldwide viewpoint. The challenges facing the modern Church are myriad: the confrontation of sexual abuse by clergy; the existential reality of climate change; the complex life issues from abortion to artificial intelligence; the gaping void between the rich and the poor; and the questions surrounding the aged; they all need a global perspective. And, of course, there were the internal Church issues in the curia, the authorities of bishops' conferences in each country, Vatican financial accountability and transparency, and what Francis called the evils of clericalism.

Vatican Financial Intrigue

One of the fundamental first items on his powerful "to do" list was the call of the conclave to clean up the Vatican finances.

Rules about money laundering and tax avoidance were areas where the embassy was attempting to arrive at an agreement with the Holy See. These matters fell in the purview of the Secretariat of State. They were not initially assigned to the soon-to-be-established

Secretariat of the Economy. In some ways, this was a matter of timing; in other ways, it was a matter of control of turf.

With the establishment of the Secretariat of the Economy, one was led to believe that the power of fiscal control and accountability would move in a new direction. Cardinal Pell, the new head of Secretariat of the Economy with a mandate from the Holy Father, clashed with many entrenched sources who petitioned the Holy Father to keep in place decades-old traditional systems of accounting and accountability. While it was obvious that the pope did not buy the old-school line, the ebb and flow of who held what power overseeing finances changed almost weekly.

Regarding the Vatican fiscal oversight, the embassy had a visit from two individuals attached to the New York Federal Reserve. My concerns, outlined by the State and Treasury before I left Washington, dealt with money laundering and tax evasion. Issues concerning the Vatican holdings of gold were never mentioned. As is often the case with most sovereign nations, much of the Vatican holdings of gold (not enormous sums) were stored in the New York Federal Reserve. The visitors were rather tightlipped about the objectives of their visit and made it very clear that we at the embassy, and I, as ambassador, had no authority over their visit though they were asking our help to arrange meetings. The mandate of the plenipotentiary ambassador was clearly being challenged, but I allowed it to ride for this brief visit unless I saw something get out of hand.

The people from the Federal Reserve were either misinformed or ignorant about protocol in a guest country. We had the sense that during the short time they had allotted for the visit, they planned to come away totally illuminated by some miracle about the Vatican's historically opaque financial dealings. They wanted to investigate the Vatican's financial management and did not want the embassy's participation in their meetings. They were possibly taken aback when, after staff dropped them off for a meeting at the Secretariat of the Economy, where they had requested that we not participate, they found that I was invited to the luncheon hosted for them by Cardinal Pell. In fact, I was seated across the table from the cardinal in an obvious place of honor. They soon learned that in the Vatican information flows from trust. I'm certain that there was more substance shared at that luncheon than what they had learned in their "private" meetings. Inside the Vatican, it is all about relationships. And the Vatican understood "protocol" very clearly.

Some of the early challenges Cardinal Pell had to deal with included the firing of the head of the Vatican Bank, Ettore Gotti Tedeschi. By way of a defense, Tedeschi later issued an open letter on the "four mysteries" that were unsolved, in Tedeschi's opinion, or unanswered, in the opinion of others. He claimed to have a dossier of correspondence and emails that could incriminate many and he referred to his firing as the "price of transparency." Clarity, or lack thereof, is only one of the elements swirling around Vatican financial intrigue.[1]

Another financial problem facing Cardinal Pell was the Administration of the Patrimony of the Holy See (APSA), which appeared particularly averse to transparency.

Based on the generally unreliable and sensationalist Italian press, APSA, which managed most of the physical assets beyond Vatican City, was undervaluing rents and property values. I have no specific insight into this matter, but it was generally accepted that there were numerous cases where an employee of the Vatican moved into an apartment and paid a moderate rental price. That price was never adjusted, even in fifty-plus years, because the property remains within the family. Rent control on steroids, squatters rights, and even mafia-occupied property plague the APSA.[2]

In 2021, after it was revealed that there appeared to be shenanigans at the Secretary of State over the distribution of Peter's Pence and some questionable investments, Pope Francis launched major changes. One was a sweep of APSA leadership and a reorganization of how major pots of money were handled.

Meanwhile, at his first year's financial report, Cardinal Pell announced that there were cash values in the multiple millions going unreported.[3] These were not misused or misspent, they were just held off the books and undisclosed. The rebuttal was that "this was the way we always did it."

One of the bright spots from the Secretariat of the Economy was the institution of an auditor general for Vatican finances. This position would bring to light all accounts. The auditor general, Libero Milone, was to have free reign and report directly to the pope. He resigned abruptly, and mysteriously, in June 2017.[4] Those who probably knew more of the reason for his resignation and those whose opinion I had grown to respect made statements that he had begun to exceed his mandate. His undercover investigations of various staffers peeled back too much at one time. And he was then encouraged to resign.

It is interesting that it was Archbishop Becciu who served as substitute, something akin to a chief operating officer of the Secretariate of State, who was the one who publicly challenged the auditor general. By summer 2020, Archbishop Becciu was removed from his position by the pope, and by summer 2021, he was indicted for financial misdealing. Certainly, there were some financial mice running for the walls.

The Bambino Gesù Children's Hospital

Bambino Gesù Children's Hospital is owned by the Holy See and sits next to the Pontifical North American College. It is just above Vatican City on the way up the Gianicolo Hill. It also has other branches in different locations around Rome.

Very early in my tenure, we heard that there were major deficits and that the Vatican had to bail out the institution. Next, we learned that two officials at the hospital—Giuseppe Profiti, the former president of the Bambino Gesù pediatric hospital, and Massimo Spina, its former treasurer—were let go. There were major morale problems among the staff and allegations that the executive management team was pushing profits over quality care.

Reports started circulating that both the president and treasurer of the hospital were indicted for channeling hospital money—estimated at more than $500,000—to renovate and expand the apartment belonging to Cardinal Bertone, the previous Vatican secretary of state.[5]

A third individual, Italian businessman Gianantonio Bandera, appeared on the scene, although he is not listed in the indictment. He was awarded the contract for Cardinal Bertone's renovations. Allegedly, it was Cardinal Bertone who recommended Bandera for the contract. Although Cardinal Bertone is not mentioned in the indictment, his association and benefit from the project suggests a conflict of interests. To make matters even more surreal, it is reported that Bandera's company was paid twice by two different Vatican offices. Evidence presented at the trial indicates that Bandera's company billed the Vatican Bank, which asked APSA to pay $500,000 to a subcontractor hired by Bandera. Later, toward the end of 2014, the Governorato informed the court that it had paid $400,000 to Bandera's company.[6]

It is hard to make this type of situation up. But I learned long ago that money and men of the cloth shouldn't mix. It is not always that clerics can't handle money, but more often, they don't have a sense of the people around them that are unscrupulous and take advantage of them regarding such matters. The mafia all too often took advantage of unsuspecting and quasi-willing clergy. The pope, himself, in June 2014, announced that members of the mafia should consider themselves excommunicated. Only a pope could say such a thing and remain safe from retaliation.

In December 2014, a Vatican prosecutor froze the accounts of three individuals: the former president of the Vatican Bank (IOR), his lawyer, and a former director general of the bank. They were charged with embezzlement of millions of euros generated from the sale of properties owned by the bank between 2001 and 2008. Allegedly, they misrepresented the value of the properties on their books and pocketed the difference between the real sale price and the officially recorded amount. It is reported that 57 million euros were involved.[7]

In 2013, the then head of the Vatican Bank, Ernst von Freyberg, uncovered the swindle. He was the one who initiated major investigations into the bank's dealings. Such investigations continue under his successor Jean-Baptiste de Franssu, a former INVESCO banker, who strives to maintain the energy of improving systems at the IOR.

Accountability and Transparency

The newly initiated Secretariat for the Economy headed by Australian Cardinal George Pell is now without a director of the stature of Cardinal Pell. Reform has slowed but not stalled. Cardinal Pell has returned to Australia to face charges of sexual abuse that he may have ignored or covered up when he served as archbishop of Melbourne. The indictment further alleges that he may have been personally involved in abuse prior to becoming archbishop.

He ended up spending jail time but was later released and acquitted after a review of evidence. He returned to the Vatican but remains without a portfolio.

When I left Rome in January 2017, however, it could be said that the issues of accountability and transparency had improved. However, there is still a long road to what we as Americans would describe as a fully accountable and transparent institution.[8] More recently, in 2019, scandals around finances again surfaced with individuals in the Secretariat of State's First Section—the Section for Relations with States—and a director of the Financial Information Authority (AIF), the financial transparency body in the Vatican.[9]

Since then, six individuals have been indicted by a Vatican court. Cardinal Becciu, former head of the First Section at the Secretariat of State; his deputy, the head of the Financial Information Authority; his deputy; and three other Italian individuals are accused of embezzlement. To date, there hasn't yet been a case that takes a high-profile cardinal to trial at the Vatican for financial crimes. However, the high-profile nature of these cases is a culmination or a direct development of Pope Francis's mandate from the conclave in 2013.

One area where we at the embassy got involved in the financial management of the Holy See was in relation to FATCA (Foreign Tax Compliance Act).

The Department of Treasury and State

Prior to leaving Washington for the Vatican, I had a meeting arranged by Sheila Carey, the very competent State Department desk person for Vatican issues, who also helped part-time with Italian affairs at the embassy. The meeting was with staff at the Department of Treasury and State who dealt with international money laundering and terrorist financing, a field I knew only a little about. The Treasury/State folks asked that I watch closely the progress, or lack thereof, regarding the Vatican's overall financial dealings.

Apparently, in 2010, the Holy See had passed "Anti-money Laundering and Financing of Terrorism" legislation. It came into effect six months later, in April 2011. By June, the Vatican had established a Financial Intelligence Authority. Its president is Swiss lawyer René Bruelhart. His previous experience in eradicating money laundering systems included work in Liechtenstein and elsewhere. He was first hired by Benedict XVI and then named president of the Financial Intelligence Authority by Pope Francis on November 19, 2014. He is the first layperson to hold such a post, a clear indication of the Vatican's desire to rid itself of bad money practices. He was a professional and paid like one. Some say he was the highest paid individual in the Vatican service.

René Bruelhart (now under indictment) and the Financial Intelligence Authority were all part of the effort started by Pope Benedict XVI to clean up and improve the level of transparency and accountability for the Vatican's finances. What systems had been in place were based on personal trust, fraught with loopholes, and hidden behind outdated traditional systems ("we have always done it this way"). These financial structures were apparently allowed to atrophy, relying far too readily on a sense that "God will watch over us."

The Vatican had asked the Committee of Experts on the Evaluation of Anti-money Laundering Measures and the Financing of Terrorism—MONEYVAL,[10] the monitoring body of the Council of Europe—to conduct an evaluation of their overall systems and laws in November 2011. The evaluation was completed in 2012. It noted that progress was made but suggested changes in the law and the need to implement improved financial systems.

Treasury and State had an interest in tracking the Holy See's financial systems in areas of possible terrorist financing and money laundering, whether witting or unwitting. This was their concern at the Vatican and elsewhere. However, given the recent history of financial events at the Vatican, their focus was sharpened.

In January 2013, the Italian Central Bank suspended all bank card payments within Vatican City, citing the Holy See's failure to implement fully the anti–money laundering legislation.[11] Essentially, this meant that all tourists visiting Vatican museums, buying Vatican stamps at the Vatican post office, purchasing food from the Vatican grocery store (supposedly open only to those employed at the Vatican and officials, such as the ambassadorial corps accredited to the Vatican), had to pay cash. This was an enormous burden.

Another ember on the fire that burned under the Department of Treasury and State was the ongoing matter of the arrest of Msgr. Nunzio Scarano.[12] In June 2013, he attempted to illegally move 20 million euros from Switzerland to Rome by private jet. He was arrested. Scarano was an employee of APSA. This added to the Treasury and State's concern regarding the Vatican's management of money.

The Foreign Accounts Tax Compliance Act (FATCA)

Arriving in Rome and totally focused now on every statement, nuance, and action that I was privy to, it was clear to me that this new pope had an agenda to clean up the Vatican's finances. His commitment flowed from the conclave, where he heard from the cardinals about the need, in no uncertain terms, to "clean it up."

Our early milestone was to get the Vatican to sign, adhere to, and abide by FATCA's terms on tax compliance for American citizens. If so implemented, it would also help with the overall anti–money laundering and anti–terrorist financing issues in the Vatican. Not every country had signed nor adhered to FATCA regulations. Under Pope Francis, however, the Vatican wanted to turn over a new and large leaf. In 2014, we entered intensive negotiations with the Holy See to explain the terms of FATCA compliance. They recognized immediately the value of being on the list of compliant countries. The Holy

See wanted to use this regulation as a keystone for other things they were trying to clean up in their financial world.

By early November 2014, we were coming down to the wire on satisfying the FATCA requirements. Marji Christian, an officer in our embassy's political unit, was the point person. Fr. Carlos Diaz at the Secretariat of State handled negotiations for the Vatican, basically by himself. The deadline for the approval was fast approaching.

The Vatican impresses many people by its majesty and treasure, but basically the internal workings of the curia are terribly under-staffed. There are many good, intelligent people, but just not enough of them. They work long hours and often find themselves with port-folios that stretch them far beyond their competencies.

Fr. Diaz was very capable, but he was alone. When it came to the crunch time in November 2014, the FATCA agreement details were not completed to Treasury's requirement. Treasury decided that the Vatican could just wait another year. This all happened during the week of Thanksgiving. The Vatican asked for an extension, as the deadline for filing was November 30. Washington wanted to go on Thanksgiving break and basically told us to hold off until next year to be accredited.

Things had become quite animated. The Vatican had just gone through the Scarano affair and the Italian Central Bank matter. Pope Francis's desire to make progress in "cleaning it up" could not be put off for another year. Regardless of whether the FATCA issue reached the Holy Father's attention, I was receiving immense pressure from the Vatican for more time to wrap up the agreement. This was an important opportunity for the Vatican to show efficiency rather than the usual postponement. On this occasion, it was the United States that seemed inert, and uncharacteristically, the Vatican was pressing to act.

At the embassy, we understood the optics and had to kick it upstairs in Washington. Thankfully, the "powers that be" saw the value of a few weeks extension and the Vatican completed all the required paperwork.

We signed the first ever agreement—not quite a treaty—between the United States government and the Holy See on June 10, 2015.

Some Loose Ends

Now some years on, I wonder whether adherence to the terms of the agreement will continue. But things are happening.

I always felt that APSA, the group that manages all Vatican owned property both inside Vatican City and extraterritorially (outside the walls of Vatican City), had an insufficient level of accountability and transparency. One wonders who sets property rents outside the walls and whether they are competitive. Bound up in longstanding family usage and maintenance, as well as traditions of open-ended occupation and leases, APSA is overly layered in bureaucracy. Just recently, it has become known that Bishop Gustavo Zanchetta from Argentina was appointed to APSA by Pope Francis following complaints about his relations with the priests of his diocese who now face allegations of sexual abuse. Although these claims have yet to be proven, they certainly complicate the pope's life and add to the cloud that hangs over APSA.

In 2018, Pope Francis appointed Bishop Nunzio Galantino, who, since December 2013, served as secretary general of the Italian Bishops Conference (CEI). It appears that Pope Francis now has his person in place and his changes will be made.

Equally, Propaganda Fide (Propagation of the faith) takes up collections in the wealthy countries across the globe and manages those funds for the benefit of the Church in less economically endowed countries. This organization has limited public accountability and outright refused to adhere to some of the accountability terms proposed by the Secretariat of the Economy once headed by Cardinal Pell.

In July 2017, when I read Massimo Franco's article in *Corriere della Sera*, I was troubled.[13] I had spent a few hours talking to him during my time as ambassador. He posited that Pope Francis's agenda to clean up the Vatican finances was going off the tracks. He tried to make the case that the next shoe to drop is the French head of the

Vatican Bank, Jean-Baptiste de Franssu. Franco predicted he would resign within twelve months. De Franssu came out of a ten-year career as head of Invesco Continental, Europe. He really didn't need the virtually volunteer job at the IOR (Vatican Bank). In fact, when I last met him in mid-2016, I had the sense that he would not stay for long. As of July 2021, he is still at the helm of the bank. This is a positive situation in my mind.

At the embassy, we had offered IOR assistance regarding ethical investing. I gave Jean-Baptiste de Franssu the guidelines we developed at CRS and offered to put his staff in touch with Georgetown and Notre Dame universities, both of which command significant investment portfolios and have experience in ethical investing. Eventually, IOR brought Scott Malpass, the vice president and chief investment officer of the University of Notre Dame, onto their board.

In 2019, the pope signed additional statutes to enhance the strength of the Vatican auditor general.[14] It remains to be seen how these invigorated powers will work out.

My belief is that the pope and his "kitchen cabinet" of nine cardinals want to make progress on accountability and transparency regarding Vatican finances, but there are indeed various intervening forces that prefer to keep things exactly as they have been for centuries. The test of time is often a positive force, but in this case, it seems to be a negative effect. Given the wide swath of critique that has enveloped the papacy recently, I can only imagine that getting back to the nitty gritty details of accountability have dropped down on the agenda.

While it appears improvements in transparency and accountability have taken place at IOR and the Financial Intelligence Agency, I have yet to read of any substantive change in the way things were done at Propaganda Fide and continue to read reports of shady dealings.

Nevertheless, I am hopeful. The challenge of the conclave, "clean it up," is daunting, but improvements appear to be happening.

5

DIPLOMACY
AND POLITICS

MANY WORLD EVENTS catapulted the embassy and the Vatican into important dialogues: the Ebola virus broke out in Liberia and Sierra Leone, where Catholic missionaries were operating; ceasefire initiatives were the goal in other African countries where Catholic leaders were on the frontlines; situations were developing constantly in Israel, Palestine, and Syria; there was the plight of Christians and other minorities; there was Russia's invasion of Ukraine; religious freedom and human rights in China; the political situation in Venezuela; and refugees, global migration, and climate change were all matters of concern for both the Vatican and the United States. Human trafficking was an issue of concern to my predecessors, and I quickly took up the baton.

Many of these issues coincided with focus areas for the Department of State. Asking the pope to mention a cause or conflict in his New Year's Day—*Urbi et Orbi*—address from St. Peter's Square or at a Wednesday Angelus could influence decisions down the road. However, it was important to be judicious and raise the issues where we felt the Holy Father's voice would resonate.

Within a week or so of our arrival, we had a luncheon at my residence for several people addressing the horrible scourge of human trafficking. They came from religious communities and Vatican offices. Most had not met each other and had limited knowledge of what the others were doing. It was an important networking occasion for all, a chance to meet heroic and intrepid folks based in Rome, and it set the stage for our embassy being at the forefront of this issue during my tenure.

A week or so later I went to my first meeting on human trafficking at the Pontifical Academy of Sciences. Its importance was raised by the fact that the pope had penned a note, which had become public, to his fellow Argentinian, Bishop Marcelo Sanchez Sorondo, the chancellor of the Pontifical Academy of Sciences (PAS), asking, "Marcelo, what are we doing about human trafficking?"

Normally, trafficking would be in the bailiwick of the Pontifical Council for the Pastoral Care of Migrants and Itinerant People. Handing the request to the PAS indicated that Pope Francis sensed that nothing was going to happen at the Pontifical Council and that he wanted to get something going. I could never determine why the Pontifical Council was considered so passive to the issue of human trafficking, but it was not an accident that he sent the note to Bishop Sorondo, clearly a man with access to the Holy Father. It was a definite sign that this issue was high on the pope's agenda.

The issue had also been reasonably high on the agenda of the State Department, where the topic was handled by the office headed by a most capable lawyer, Luis C. de Baca, who held a credible international reputation and was most willing to share his insights and perspectives.

South Sudan

On Christmas Eve 2013, we received an urgent request from Washington, D.C. The State Department hoped we could get the Holy Father to appeal to the belligerent forces in South Sudan to back down.

I knew South Sudan well from my time with CRS, where I had once served as Africa regional director. Consequently, I knew the basic history, the players, and the horror that had accompanied many years of civil war against the North. I understood the tensions among and between the different ethnicities and was privileged to be part of the official U.S. delegation to the independence celebrations in Juba on July 9, 2011. All the world had high hopes for this new nation.

But soon after that great day, the situation between President Salva Kiir and his deposed Vice President Riek Machar became explosive. Thousands were caught in a power struggle. Each rallied his respective ethnic group and staked his claim to the presidency.

Kiir, whom I had once met, is a Catholic, and the hope was that, if the pope inserted himself as a mediator, there might be a possibility of calming the situation.

So, with great zeal and determination I attempted to email various folks in the Secretariat of State and elsewhere. (It was still early enough in my tenure that folks in the Vatican had not yet shared their personal mobile telephone numbers.) December 24 is a holiday at the Vatican: many go home, and others catch up quietly on backlogged paperwork. It became clear that it would take time to build the relationships of trust. But nonetheless I was energized.

There's the old-fashioned diplomatic way of talking to people. I went to midnight Mass at St. Peter's that evening. Afterward, on our way out, I approached Archbishop Dominique Mamberti, the then secretary for relations with states (the number two in the Secretariat) who was standing beside his under secretary, Msgr. Antoine Camilleri. The archbishop said, "I understand you tried to contact the Secretariat of State today," as he continued to greet diplomats departing from the Mass.

I explained the matter briefly and asked if it would be possible for the pope to call either President Kiir or Vice President Machar and ask if either could back down their hostilities. I said that I had the private cell phones for each and would be pleased to provide the pope with them. Msgr. Camilleri accepted.

Whether or not the calls were made, I don't know, but the next day at the pope's *Urbi et Orbi* address in St. Peter's Square, he called for peace in Sudan, reaching an audience of millions via television and Vatican Radio. Fighting continued for the next three years with thousands of dead and millions displaced, but nevertheless a light was directed briefly to the conflict for the world to take notice.

It was an important lesson for a newbie diplomat: zealousness is not necessarily the wisest path to reach your desired destination. At that Christmas Mass just two and a half months after I presented my credentials, I held only limited credibility, something that can only be built over time.

South Sudan retained an important place on the Vatican's agenda. There was considerable chatter about the pope's desire to visit South Sudan during my tenure, but given the problem of security, it proved impossible. It was suggested that it might even be a joint visit with the archbishop of Canterbury. What eventually did happen was an invitation to President Kiir and opposition leader Riek Machar to visit the Vatican, meet with the pope, and participate in a spiritual retreat with Archbishop Welby in 2019.

Geopolitical Equations

Venezuela

The Holy See has a broad and long assessment of most geopolitical situations in the world. Many sources feed into their assessments. No matter how important the issue, an insistent American ambassador is just going to be one of many, albeit weighty, considerations of the Holy See.

But there were other issues where an ambassador can inform thinking on current events. I asked Ambassador Tom Shannon, who was then under secretary for political affairs and a noted expert on Latin America, to come and discuss the situation in Venezuela with Cardinal Parolin. The cardinal had served as the apostolic nuncio in Caracas before taking up the post as secretary of state. Their conversations were rich.

One of Ambassador Shannon's requests was to ask whether the Holy See could use its "good offices" to mediate between President Maduro and the opposition. The Vatican Secretary of State was not averse to playing a more direct intermediary role in Venezuela's problems but insisted that both President Maduro and a united opposition had to request publicly that the Vatican play such a role. Eventually, such requests were forthcoming, and the Vatican sent Archbishop Celli, a very experienced diplomat. He determined that the situation was not ready for a settlement nor an agreement despite the formal request from both parties.

Nuclear Weapons

The Holy See was also contemplating its posture and position on nuclear deterrence and nuclear weapons in general.[1] This decision, we realized, had been in process for some time, certainly back to 2010 when Archbishop Celestino Migliore took an opposing position when he served as the apostolic nuncio and permanent observer of the Holy See to the United Nations, in New York. Aware of that reality, I wanted the Holy See to understand our position on both deterrence and nonproliferation.

Ambassador Rose Gottemoeller gave a presentation during my orientation in Washington before leaving for the Vatican. She was the under secretary for state as well as the assistant secretary of state for verification, compliance, and implementation. Her presentation prompted me to invite her to come and speak to those at the Vatican engaged in the issues of arms control, nuclear deterrence, and nuclear nonproliferation.

She came twice and the curia officials said they found it helpful, but after I departed Rome, the Holy Father took a more strident position opposing nuclear deterrence.

The Red Line in Syria

Syria was boiling during my time at the Vatican. The red line had been crossed, but we did not strike. Rather, an agreement was reached with the support of many parties including Russia to take the chemical weapons away from the Assad regime. But that still left ISIS in control of significant territory in Syria. This was a complicated geopolitical equation. Admittedly, I could not adequately explain nor was I suitably versed on our posture, so I invited General John Allen, the special presidential envoy to the global coalition to counter ISIL,[2] to visit and explain our approach to the Secretariat of State. He brilliantly unveiled a five-point program, the majority of which had nothing to do with guns. I believed he eased a lot of the anxiety of many in the Vatican who may have felt that this could have been a repeat of the takedown of Saddam Hussein. He changed a few minds at the Secretariat of State. In fact, two days after this meeting, Archbishop Silvano Tomasi, permanent observer of the Holy See to the United Nations and Specialized Organization in Geneva, Switzerland, issued a statement that the Vatican condoned the use of force against ISIS.

Ukraine

Many of us were also frustrated that the Holy See would not take a more forceful position against the Russian invasion of Ukraine and the takeover of Crimea. The Ukrainian ambassador tried her best to elicit a more public and supportive statement from the Holy See. She was not successful, though some of us, including the Polish, Lithuanian, and British ambassadors, tried to support her. In my case, I invited Geoff Pyatt, our then ambassador to Ukraine, from Kiev on two occasions to brief at the Secretariat of State and other offices, such as the Office for Interreligious Dialogue, whose officers were well familiar with the Catholic-Orthodox tension in Ukraine. I also invited Kathleen Kavalec, who served as the director for Russian affairs in the Bureau of Europe and Eurasian Affairs, to offer a lucid and trenchant picture of Russia's motivations in Ukraine and elsewhere.

However, it was not until Cardinal Parolin made a visit to Ukraine, Lithuania, and Latvia and experienced firsthand the Russian jets flying low over a site he was touring that there was some change in the Vatican's public position.

Of course, the Ukrainian issue was intertwined with the Vatican's position with the Russian Orthodox Church and their sense of propriety and control over their Ukrainian Orthodox adherents. But what was hard to fathom was the fact the young archbishop of the Ukrainian Greek Catholic Church, Sviatoslav Shevchuk, was a close friend of Pope Francis. He had been stationed in Buenos Aires when Pope Francis was archbishop there and was a frequent visitor to Rome and to our residence, often bringing some of his bishops.

The Ukrainian Greek Catholic Church had also been charged by the Russian Orthodox Church with encroaching on the territory and adherents of the Orthodox Church. Consequently, relations between the Vatican and the Orthodox Church, particularly the Russian Orthodox Church, were complex.

Cuba

I must admit that we were surprised by the pope's visit to Cuba as a prelude to his trip to the United States. After we first interpreted it to Washington as a symbolic gesture following the path of Christianity into North America, we later learned that Pope Francis had planned an historic meeting with Patriarch Kirill in Havana.[3]

There was speculation in certain quarters in the Vatican and among the diplomatic community that it was a surprise meeting organized by Cardinal Koch of the Pontifical Council for Promoting Christian Unity without the assent of the Secretary of State, but I doubt that this was the case.

The pope and the patriarch signed an agreement in Havana that was somewhat controversial as it appeared to favor the Orthodox, but nonetheless, the meeting itself was filled with symbolism in that it was a first meeting between a pope and a Russian patriarch.

On October 19, 1960, the Eisenhower administration imposed economic sanctions on the Castro regime in Cuba. I was thirteen years old. For the prior eight years, during the height of the Cold War, the religious sisters at school were instructing us on how to hide under our desks in preparation for a Russian attack, which seemed a near certainty. We assumed that the godless communists were set on propagating an anti-Christian ideology on clear-minded American Catholics.

Such was the talk among the kids of West Roxbury, whether we were playing hockey on the frozen Turtle Pond or baseball at Billings Field. In the 1950s, we were the good guys; they were the bad guys. Eisenhower had just made clear that Cuba and Castro were on the side of the bad guys. End of story.

It continued, virtually unquestioned by many, for decades. But it was during his first presidential campaign that candidate Barack Obama began positing the idea that sanctions on Cuba had little effect, other than allowing the Cuban government to blame Americans for all of Cuba's problems—including shortages of consumer goods and the lack of economic opportunity. Moreover, the looming threat of a hostile United States ninety miles to the north was used to explain the necessity for total government control over all aspects of life.

Though this was not a major part of Obama's campaign, it was clear that he believed that it was time to change the United States' policy toward Cuba.

I was lucky to know a bit more than most about the situation there. My first visit to Cuba was in 1994 as Catholic Relief Services had started a program supporting Caritas Cuba in 1993. The Soviet Union had long propped up the Cuban government and economy and, when the Soviet economy collapsed in the early 1990s, things got terribly hard for the Cuban people because the Soviet Union severely cut back assistance to Cuba.

Even after decades of rule by those "godless" communists that we so feared back in grammar school, the Church retained an important presence in Cuban society. Caritas had succeeded in providing medical assistance in areas where the Cuban government found difficulty. The result was that CRS held one, if not the only, U.S. Treasury permits to ship humanitarian assistance to the island. That gave us some degree of access to, and approbation from, the Cuban government.

Consequently, I was not ignorant of the relationship between our two governments. In fact, in 1998, at the request of the journalist Scott Armstrong, the coauthor with Bob Woodward of *The Brethren*,[4] I met Peter Angelos, the majority owner of the Baltimore Orioles, who was attempting to facilitate a game between the Orioles and the Cuban national baseball team. I never fully understood Armstrong's engagement other than as a facilitator and a potential author of a book on baseball. He did, however, realize that we at CRS had access to the Cuban government and the Treasury Department—something that was unique at that time. In the end, Angelos didn't need us, as the U.S. government gave the Orioles permission to play in Havana and allowed the Cuban team to play a very well-attended reciprocal game in Baltimore.[5] The fact that all this was needed simply to play a couple of baseball games was yet another example of the awkward and cumbersome embargo with a country so close to our shores. For a neighbor that shares our national pastime along with so much mutual history, it all seemed such an anomaly.

The United States and Cuba

There were many narratives that emerged from President Obama's visit to the Vatican in March 2014, a very special occasion for all involved, including me and my embassy team. The visit wiped out the talking point that the Obama administration was downgrading its relations with the Holy See and the Catholic Church, and it showed that there was much common ground between the two states and the two leaders. To the chagrin of some so-called Vatican pundits who got it wrong, it became clear that the personal relationship between the Holy Father and President Obama was warm.

All of us in the party accompanying the president waited rather awkwardly, standing about in the anteroom as the pope and president met. It's hard to make simple small talk for an hour when you're with the secretary of state, the national security advisor and her deputy, Ben Rhodes, and a few others. One cannot talk policy in a public setting, and there is only so much Archbishop Ganswein can elaborate on with just the view out one window. However, when the question about Pope Benedict XVI came up, he sparkled. He was and remains very close to Pope Benedict.

We at the embassy were not privy to the meeting between the two leaders. It was an issue on "very close hold." In hindsight, I believe that the issue of Cuba took up a significant portion of their time together. I also suppose that the situations in the Ukraine and Middle East peace were also discussed.

Every other country in the Western Hemisphere had reached an accommodation with Cuba. So, it was no surprise that this pope from Argentina was very familiar with the Church in Cuba and the issues swirling around that country's estranged relationships with the United States, and that he would certainly be inclined to support an improvement in relations between the two countries. In fact, in 1998, he had written a short book, *Dialogues between Pope John Paul II and Fidel Castro*.[6] He had been asked to accompany Pope John Paul II during his visit to Cuba and was conversant with the issues in Cuba and, as the book reveals, not sympathetic to the Cuban government's Marxist line.

Furthermore, there were many around him that either had direct experience in Cuba or dealt with it on a regular basis. Archbishop Giovanni Becciu, the *sostituto*, or deputy, of the Vatican Secretariat of State had been apostolic nuncio in Havana; Msgr. Antoine Camilleri, the under secretary at the second section of the Secretariat of State, had served in the Havana nunciature. Archbishop Beniamino Stella, the soon-to-be prefect/head of the Congregation for Clergy, had also been apostolic nuncio in Havana; Cardinal Marc Ouellet, prefect of the Congregation for Bishops and the president of the Commission for Latin America; Cardinal Sean O'Malley, the archbishop of Boston; Cardinal Oscar Rodriguez Maradiaga, archbishop of Tegucigalpa, Honduras, and secretary of the Council of Nine Advisors; and by the time of the president's visit, Cardinal Pietro Parolin, who had recently returned from a few years as apostolic nuncio in Venezuela—all of them knew Cuba well.

It would be safe to assume that their reaction to a suggestion that the Vatican play a role in talks between the United States and Cuba would have been positive, maybe even joyous. Obviously, Cardinal Jaime Ortega in Havana would have been very supportive. So, most likely the issue arose during that March 2014 meeting with Obama.[7]

On December 15, 2014, I was attending a meeting with Cardinal Parolin and Secretary of State Kerry. As the conversation transitioned from a discussion on Middle East peace to Cuba, Secretary

Kerry outlined for the secretary of state what was to happen with the president's announcement on a change in U.S. policy toward Cuba and a prisoner exchange, plus the release of Alan Gross, the American Aid worker jailed by Cuban security.

When the beginning of the process of normalizing relations between the two countries was announced on December 17, the media was keen to know Pope Francis's role, and how and when the Vatican became involved. I couldn't say anything because, of course, I really didn't know anything beyond my informed speculation. (Although earlier in the year, we had asked for the Holy See's intervention on the release of Alan Gross.) There was also an inkling of change before December 17, when, after a Sistine Chapel Christmas concert, the Cuban ambassador seated inexplicably behind me (seating was generally done by date of presentation of credentials) made a special effort to shake my hand and wish me a Merry Christmas in English.

The media was certain that the pope's role was vital. I am certain that it was, but the entire affair was an example of how saying less always telegraphs more to the media, giving them abundant grist for speculation.

Many wished to proclaim a role in the rapprochement, among them, the Community of Sant'Egidio. Cuba was one of the places where they had established a small but vibrant local community.

By the time President Obama and Castro announced the thaw in relations, Sant'Egidio had a history in Cuba, working quietly behind the scenes to try to do what they could to foster peaceful relationships and support Church communities in the country.

Two months after the announced thaw, the Community of Sant'Egidio celebrated the forty-seventh anniversary of its founding with a Mass at the magnificent St. John Lateran Archbasilica, the pope's cathedral as Bishop of Rome. All the diplomatic community accredited to the Holy See were always invited to these anniversary Masses. We attended each one, as did most ambassadors and those associated with the Community in Rome. This time, the crowd inside was very large.

As we arrived, Joan and I were met at the entrance by an individual from the Community whom we knew well and who personally ushered us to the second row of the reserved diplomatic section. No sooner had we been seated in our appointed places, however, then Dr. Domenico Giani, an Italian security expert who was the inspector general of the Corpo della Gendarmeria, moved us to the front row. He was overseeing security, since this church, although a distance from Vatican City, is part of the Holy See.

It became clear what was happening: the Sant'Egidio folks wanted me seated next to the Cuban ambassador, Alejandro Lopez Clemente. Our wives were seated directly behind us.

It was a staged photo op. Since Cardinal Jaime Ortega, the cardinal archbishop of Havana, was celebrating the Mass and offering the homily, this was a perfect chance for the Community to provide the world with an image of rapprochement at the Sant' Egidio anniversary Mass with the American and Cuban ambassadors seated next to each other.

Sadly, Ambassador Clemente passed away about six months later. But he had witnessed the change, and I am glad that we had this wonderful occasion together.

The fifty years of estrangement seemed to end overnight. In reality, long, hard discussions and proposals to iron out problems behind closed doors culminated in an agreement. There are always detractors, as with every change. When the cameras spotlighted us in the front row at the "kiss of peace" portion of the Mass, few failed to notice that we were, ironically, surrounded by Vatican gendarmerie. They sat close enough to us so as not to be able to conceal their bulging side arms.

Guantanamo Bay

Though not directly involving the Cuban government, one other issue in which the embassy got involved with the Vatican was over the prisoners at Guantanamo.

At the beginning of 2002, the United States began transferring "enemy combatants" to the prison at Guantanamo Bay in Cuba. The prison is run by the U.S. Navy and was established by an agreement with the government of Cuba in the early 1900s. President Obama had made a campaign pledge to close the prison.

In the summer of 2014, I received a request from Cliff Sloan, the special envoy for closing Guantanamo Bay, asking that the Holy See go on the record as being supportive of the closure and the transfer of prisoners to third countries. In particular, he felt that if the Vatican expressed a positive attitude toward the release, the Catholic bishops in Chile and Colombia would also be receptive to the transfers. Washington thought that they already had a positive environment in Uruguay to transfer four individuals, but they wanted more assurances. I counseled that they should approach the president of Episcopal Conference of Uruguay in Montevideo if there was hesitation. However, Envoy Sloan countered that the Ministry of Foreign Affairs in Uruguay was concerned about leaks. Obviously, accepting prisoners from the Guantanamo Bay Naval Base (also called GTMO) had sharp political dimensions locally.

I raised the matter with the Vatican Secretariat of State, whose position was clear. They would support the principle of prisoner release on "humanitarian grounds," but the local bishops' conferences had to have the ability to make their own decisions.

At times, the local bishops want Vatican guidance, and at other times, they see the Vatican as interfering. In the case of Uruguay, they wanted Vatican guidance and a solution was worked out. Uruguay accepted six prisoners.

I don't believe the same negotiations succeeded in Chile or Colombia.

Upon my return to the United States for the State Department's "Chief of Mission" (U.S. ambassadors worldwide) conference the following March, I held a meeting with Cliff and his team and quickly inventoried the world as to which countries might be willing to accept prisoners. At least, we had clarity on the Holy See's position. At times, it was most helpful, as was the case in Uruguay, but not always.

6

POPE FRANCIS VISITS THE UNITED STATES

IMMEDIATELY FOLLOWING the president's trip to meet the pope in March 2014, all of us at the embassy began anticipating and planning for a reciprocal papal trip to the United States. The invitation had been extended by the president, but what most people, including the folks at the curia, would say was that "the Holy Father always says that he would love to visit your country." And he does, but the pressures of schedule, time, and health just doesn't allow every wish. Trips had to be strategic, and the papal visit to the United States was certainly strategic for many reasons.

My intuitive, "gut" feeling was that it was going to happen and that it would happen on my watch. There was a special rapport that emanated from the private session between the pope and the president in March 2014. The convergence of interests—Cuba, climate change, eliminating poverty, Human Rights, refugees, Middle East peace—were but a few items that brought them together and it seemed inevitable that this would generate a visit.

All reports indicated that Pope Francis had never been to the United States. So, the fact that this would be his first visit was notable. In our minds, we began to posit the major concerns: Where? How long? Would he speak in Spanish or English? Could he get the U.S. American zeitgeist? Who would he meet with other than those in the White House? Would the occasion of the World Meeting of Families in Philadelphia be the reason for his visit?

Trips were scheduled by a team led by Dr. Alberto Gasbarri, the administrative director of Vatican Radio and coordinator of papal travel. There were other decision makers in the arrangements, but Dr. Gasbarri was the person who surveyed the chosen locations and determined what was doable and what was not. Dr. Gasbarri has an encyclopedic memory, an engineer's attention to detail, a refreshing ability, rare for curial officials, to tell you straight "that will not be possible," and a good sense of humor.

He and his team do the preliminaries as well as the follow-ups. They visit the country, meet with the local bishops' conference, the apostolic nuncio, and the local church offices that might host the Holy Father and scope out every step of the visit. In the case of the United States, he meets with the Office of the Chief of Protocol in the Department of State, the Protocol and Liaison Service for the United Nations, and the Archdioceses of Washington, New York, and Philadelphia. But he does not deal with the security matters.

Security was dealt with by Dr. Domenico Giani. I had many cordial meetings with Dr. Giani; however, the least pleasant was the meeting to review the papal trip to the United States that we will discuss later.

The Three Dimensions of the Papal Visit

This visit needed to be understood on three dimensions: the pope vis-à-vis the United States; the pope vis-à-vis the cities and populations he would visit; and the pope vis-à-vis his message. A major factor was how he would "play" in America. As early as 2014, he was already being characterized in some quarters as a Latin American socialist, even anti–United States. He had made a few flubs in speaking about women, which had not been well received in the United States, and would compromise his credibility and the Obama administration's association with his agenda. Could he capture the imagination of Americans, having never been there?

One way I chose to address the first dimensional issue was to offer some current literature to help with the rhetoric he would use. When I met the individuals whom I believed were planning the substance of the trip, I offered them two books that I had recently read. The first was Paul Elie's *The Life You Save May Be Your Own*, a biography of Dorothy Day, Thomas Merton, Flannery O'Conner, and Walker Percy.[1] The second book was *The Road to Character* by David Brooks that also speaks to important and notable individuals who shaped American character.[2]

The second dimension was concerned with where the pope would go and to whom he would speak. The World Meeting of Families, a triennial event held in different locations around the world, was definite. The event is promoted by the Office of Laity, Family and Life. Pope Benedict had agreed to attend the event in Philadelphia, and Pope Francis decided to honor that commitment. Since he would be in Philly, could a quick visit across the border to Camden, one of our nation's most challenged cities, be included? That would place him among those who were economically distressed and of special concern to him. The White House suggested Chicago, to move away from the Northeast. I heard from bishops and politicians across the nation who suggested, "Tell him to come to California. If he is going to canonize Fr. Junipero Serra, he should do it in California." Another suggestion was to come to the border with Mexico. "It would be a poignant way to address the migrant issues."

I shared many of these suggestions, but the Vatican planners were also hearing directly from mayors, governors, bishops, and communities.

The third dimension was the substance of the pope's message. As the visit became a reality and the locations became firmer, a couple of things happened. First, the release of the environmental encyclical,

Laudato Si'—just four months before the trip—created an agenda of its own. It elevated the attention to the pope and his voice on the global stage both within and beyond the administration. Second, the White House wanted to maximize the impact of the Holy Father's visit with the confirmation of a set of mutual agreeable items. This second item took some managing.

The White House Involvement

The organization of the agenda for the pope's visit for the White House was given to Dr. Charles Kupchan, the senior director for Europe at the National Security Council (NSC), who was assisted by Dr. Melissa Rogers, the director of the White House office of Faith-Based and Community Initiatives. Melissa was intelligent and willing to learn what she didn't know. My first encounter with Charles's assistants, however, was more difficult. He was an expert on Eastern Europe and Russia, but he and his assistants knew little if anything about the Vatican.

They wanted to have a teleconference with some leadership at the Secretariat of State wherein they would be able to hash out a mutually agreeable set of "deliverables" that the White House could announce. My initial response was that the Secretariat of State did not do teleconferences. Second, they most probably would not accept a list of deliverables. I got heavy pushback from the folks at the White House who insisted that it had to be done this way.

I dutifully made the request at the level of Foreign Minister Archbishop Paul Gallagher, with whom I had a very good and longstanding relationship stretching back to the '90s, when I served with CRS in Manila, where he served at the nunciature. He gave me the already predicted answer that the Vatican does not do teleconferences. It was neither the norm nor did they want the risk of misunderstanding while speaking with a group of individuals in a teleconference, some of whom are not even seen on the screen.

Furthermore, for the Vatican, the visit was the "message," and there was, from their perspective, no necessity in framing some agreed-upon points. The Washington, White House, and Congress segments of the trip were not about transactional items.

Archbishop Gallagher's suggestion was that if they wanted to come and speak personally about the visit, the door was open.

I passed along the message, which was found to be unacceptable. The NSC folks continued to press the video teleconference idea until I had to kick my concerns up to the White House chief of staff, who eased the tension. Dr. Kupchan and Dr. Rogers came to the Vatican.

Their visit proved auspicious and informative. The White House team left Rome pleased and with expectations that were reasonable. I believe both organizers also left with a deeper appreciation that the Holy See had ways of doing things and approaches to both diplomacy and the management of the Holy Father's persona that were not framed in a four-year term of office but had a far longer horizon. His persona had a far greater global perspective than one might find in a head of state of Estonia, Ghana, Poland, or any other country.

In April 2015, the Vatican announced a pre-U.S. trip to Havana to meet with President Castro. This, of course, added another focus of interest on the Holy Father. Arriving in the United States by the historical route of its discovery when there were no borders offered a subtle but clear symbolism.

The Media

Once the visit was officially announced, *National Geographic* proposed to do a feature issue on Pope Francis. They sought our help in arranging a meeting with Vatican individuals who might facilitate the proper contacts and approvals. I contacted Greg Burke, my American golfing friend, who was handling communication in the second section of the Secretariat of State. He directed me to the now Bishop Paul Tighe, at the time the secretary of the Pontifical Council for Social Communications. There was some hesitancy, but the then Msgr. Tighe said that he would be agreeable to at least talking with representatives from *National Geographic*.

A lunch meeting was set up at my residence with Archbishop Claudio Celli; Msgr. Paul Tighe, his deputy; Susan Goldberg, the editor-in-chief of *National Geographic*; Robert Draper, a well-known writer; and David Yoder, the photographer. *National Geographic* wanted the opportunity to "shadow" the pope and cover his daily steps in both literary and photographic media.

After extensive negotiations, they received access to most of Pope Francis's public events and liturgies, with David Yoder visible at many liturgies from May through August 2015. I do not know how much time Robert Draper was allowed, but suggest he did one of the finer profiles on Pope Francis. I was proud that we could offer an opportunity for the first meeting.

60 Minutes

Finally, the trip was on. Peter Martin, our capable political officer, Antoinette Hurtado, the equally capable media person, and Joan and I left for the United States. Antoinette had arranged significant publicity in Rome prior to the trip—more than two dozen interviews. I did, with some initial hesitation, an interview with Scott Pelley on *60 Minutes*.[3] I feared a Mike Wallace "gotcha" style interview, but Scott Pelley was both a gentleman and honestly interested in learning my perspective on the pope. Some local interviews that I did were welcomed by Vatican public affairs staff, who appreciated sharing the burden of the many requests for information on the trip.

Finally, the groundwork in Rome was completed.

The White House Prebriefing

At this time, the foreign service officer at the U.S. Department of State for the Vatican was Sonia Tarantolo. She informed me that I was to go for a "prebrief" at the White House. There were so many code words and no time to ask what they meant. I presumed that this was protocol regarding where to stand, file, and be seated at the event on the South Lawn. Joan asked me if she should come and I said, "No, it was just about placements and seating." I walked over to the White House from the hotel, which was six blocks away. I went through the security and was ushered up to the main entrance. I was seated by the receptionists.

Some minutes later, a gentleman came and introduced himself as Michael Carpenter, the vice president's chief of staff. He told me I shouldn't be nervous. With that guidance, I was. I was brought into the vice president's office. He rose from his desk to greet me and offered the couch in front of his desk. The room was populated with about a dozen others. Very quickly, I changed gears as I realized that *I was the briefing.*

After lengthy pleasantries, he asked, "Well, ambassador, I am going to chair the meeting with Cardinal Parolin. Which way should we take the discussion?" The large group around me immediately reminded me of how small the Vatican group would be. I told him that Cardinal Parolin's delegation was going to be composed of four people: the secretary of state, the foreign minister, the substitute for general affairs in the Secretariat, and the apostolic nuncio to the United States. If the vice president's delegation was much larger, there would be little conversation. I had learned the veep's delegation was going to be nine. He immediately asked his staff, "Why so many?" When he got no answer, he said, "We will have to have a 'come-to-Jesus' discussion on that matter."

The second suggestion I offered Vice President Biden was that he should open with some questions on Cuba, since Cardinal Parolin and his team had just come from there.

On the day of the meeting, those present were the vice president, Secretary Kerry, Ben Rhodes, Charlie Kupchan, Melissa Rogers, and me. The Vatican delegation was four. The conversation opened and remained about Cuba, for the most part, until the door opened, and only then, we discussed Venezuela for the last few minutes.

Pope Francis Arrives

The pope's arrival was scheduled at what was once called Andrews Air Force Base, now Joint Base Andrews. There were about thirty of us gathered in the base lounge. The head of protocol for the White House and the State Department, Ambassador Peter Selfridge, and his team lined us up according to protocol in the order in which we would greet the pope at the steps of the plane. When the plane was on approach, we followed our instructions and trooped out to the tarmac in our designated order.

The greeting group consisted of the president and his family; the vice president and his family; the base commander of Andrews; Cardinal Wuerl of the Archdiocese of Washington, D.C., the apostolic nuncio, Archbishop Vigano, followed by Joan and me. Joan has a distinct recollection that after the plane touched down, there were a few gentle rains, and just before the door opened, a gust of wind so strong that the women had to hold their hair and dresses. The plane taxied in very slowly and had already come to a stop, so it was not blowback from the engines, but rather an unexplained gust.

It was a wonderful welcome, with the pope smiling with genuine joy, and all of the greeting party clearly so pleased to have him in the United States. After two years of preparation, it was happening.

The Archdiocese of Washington had arranged for some high schoolers from surrounding Catholic schools to greet and cheer his arrival. They were exuberant and very vocal. They became ecstatic when President Obama broke ranks and shook hands with them through the barriers.

At the airport we had the first view of the Fiat Cinque Cento (500) that the pope would ride in during the trip. The Secret Service had encouraged him to ride in an armored vehicle; he turned that suggestion down. It was quite an image, this tiny Fiat surrounded by the black armored Chevrolet Suburbans for the United States contingent, each large enough to fit his Fiat within them. After all the greetings, the convoy left Andrews Air Force Base for the papal nunciature on Massachusetts Avenue in downtown Washington, D.C. On the way into town, there were the requisite protesters on one corner with their signs about priest abuse and slogans that read "The pope is the devil," and a range of other concerns. But on every street, the numbers of jubilant supporters far surpassed the small groups of protesters. Thousands welcomed Pope Francis with great energy and love.

Before we entered the motorcade, I greeted Cardinal Pietro Parolin, the secretary of state, and Archbishop Paul Gallagher, the foreign minister, who accompanied the Holy Father. Behind them I reached out to greet Dr. Domenico Giani. He was not happy, telling me in no uncertain terms that things were not going well. He mentioned that even while in Cuba, he was receiving reports that changes were being made to plans that had been explicitly agreed upon.

Papal Security

In this new environment of terrorist threats and after the attack on Pope John Paul II, protection of the pope now falls on the Directorate for Security Services and Civil Protection, which includes the Gendarmerie Corps and the Fire Department. The Directorate is headed currently by Dr. Giani.

The Swiss Guard maintains protection inside Vatican City, complementing the security provided by the gendarmerie and serves a ceremonial role in public liturgies and events as well as inside the apostolic palace.

Essentially, the gendarmerie serves as the police department, the secret service, the FBI, and the CIA combined. They also manage the Vatican prison, which houses a few inmates. They protect the Holy Father whether he is inside Vatican City, somewhere in Rome, or outside Rome. They also handle intelligence and security preparations for all the pope's trips and run beside his car whenever he is moving.

Well trained and deeply committed, the gendarmerie are recruited from the Italian military or various Italian police forces. Dr. Giani was an officer in the Guardia di Finanza, the militarized branch of the Italian police dealing with financial crimes, smuggling, and illegal drugs. It is a coveted honor to be accepted into the Gendarmerie

Corps of Vatican City State. They are often in plain clothes at certain events outside Vatican City. In fact, Dr. Giani, himself, is often at the side of the "Popemobile" when the Holy Father moves about St. Peter's Square after liturgical events.

Dr. Giani had been with the gendarmerie since 1999 and was inspector general of the Corpo della Gendarmeria, and the chief bodyguard of Popes Benedict XVI and Francis from June 3, 2006, to October 14, 2019. For him, his role and position were a religious vocation.

At the embassy, we dealt with him on several occasions. When we were working to free hostages in Iran, Syria, and other places where he had contacts and we were limited, he was generous with information and interventions, and his contacts were solid, honed over many years. Often, we could offer him our own information or services, so it was a mutually beneficial arrangement.

While the Holy See was interested in the general welfare of all, understandably there were specific cases they focused on, such as the abductions of Fr. Paolo Dall'Oglio, an Italian Jesuit priest, who was working in Syria, and Fr. Tom Uzhunnalil, an Indian Salesian priest (since released), who was working with the Missionaries of Charity in Yemen.

We also dealt with Dr. Giani on the visits of important American officials from the administration and Congress. He was always helpful in securing access.

When we were getting ready for the pope's visit to the United States, Joseph Clancy, the head of the United States Secret Service, came to Rome. He and Dr. Giani had already developed a warm relationship—so close that Clancy once brought his sick and dying father to the Vatican and Dr. Giani arranged for a personal audience with Pope Francis.

Pope Francis's visit to the United States also spurred visits from the director of the FBI, James Comey, and later Lisa Monaco, who served as the advisor for Homeland Security under President Obama and currently serves as deputy attorney general of the United States. Her portfolio was broad and involved substantive and solid discussions with Dr. Giani.

Change of Security Plans

The preparations for the papal trip to the United States in 2015 brought Dr. Giani to the United States twice. He ironed out the entire agenda planned by Dr. Gasbarri, the principal coordinator for papal travel, and ran through the multiple security scenarios. Details such as exactly where each car would be, who would be in them, where the Holy Father would stay, and the precise security protocols for each locale were all written into an agreement between the United States and Vatican security entities. In fact, it was signed by the Holy Father.

When Pope Francis's plane touched down at Andrews Air Force Base on September 23, 2015, Dr. Giani came down the ramp to the tarmac looking hot and tired. I greeted him saying, *Benvenuto, va tutto bene?* (Welcome, how's everything going?). Dr. Giani replied quickly and curtly, "No." I knew then that I was in for something interesting.

Over the next two days, I learned of all that he considered to be a total breach of the agreement he and the pope had signed with the Secret Service on procedures and security protocols. For example, once he settled the Holy Father into the nunciature (the Vatican Embassy) on Massachusetts Avenue, he and his deputy went for a walk. Upon returning to the nunciature, both he and his deputy were body searched. He felt this was a personal affront. There were other incidents as well. Agreements about security barriers at the nunciature and other access issues were ignored or overturned despite specific agreements.

The complaints continued over the next three days as the papal delegation moved to New York.

In New York, the pope was lodged at the nunciature on Seventy-Second Street, but the rest of the official delegation—Cardinal Parolin, Archbishop Gallagher, and Archbishop Vigano—were lodged at a hotel closer to the United Nations. The Secret Service or other security forces at play—and there were many—decided that the delegation could not join the pope at the entrance to the United Nations. If they came to join him at the nunciature, they would be required to wait in their vehicles for approximately forty-five minutes.

I called Joe Clancy, the director of the Secret Service, to ask what was happening, passing along the concerns of Dr. Giani. With a sense of resignation, he told me that this had become a "national security event" and as such, there were many more security agencies engaged and most had not been party to—or even knew about—the Secret Service agreement with the Vatican. I was sure that I would get the full brunt of the complaints when I got back to Rome; meanwhile all these problems occupied a great deal of my time and attention. They were unknown to anyone outside internal security, including the pope. Indeed, despite such difficulties, things went very well.

Pope Francis at the White House

The morning following the arrival at Joint Base Andrews, we gathered in the Roosevelt Room at the White House. Joan and I were there with most of the Cabinet secretaries and their spouses, along with some invited guests, mingling for about a half hour. We chatted with some of those who had visited the Vatican and whom we had hosted at the Ambassador's Residence, including Jeh Johnson, the then secretary of homeland security and his wife; Gina McCarthy, the then administrator of the Environmental Protection Agency, and her husband; Ethel Kennedy and her son; House Leader Nancy Pelosi; and many others. Many wanted a primer on Pope Francis; others took the occasion to explain their major concerns to us, hoping that we could carry them to the Vatican.

We were finally escorted to the South Lawn, where Cabinet members were seated on the right of the stage. We were with the group on the left. A huge crowd filled the lawn leading down the Ellipse. The Washington Monument towered in the background reflecting an exceptionally beautiful day.

After about fifteen minutes, the pope arrived in his little Fiat at the White House entrance on the South Lawn in front of us. It was an incongruous image that I will never forget: the president of the United States greeting Pope Francis stepping out of his Fiat in front of the White House. The United States Marine Band playing a welcome tribute and a military honor guard standing at attention. As the president and first lady greeted the pope, the ever-present Msgr. Mark Miles, the translator, rushed around behind the Fiat to provide his services.

The pope appeared stiff and maybe uncomfortable during the military welcome on the South Lawn. But when it was his turn to speak, he seemed at ease talking in English and gave a memorable speech, making two powerful points.[4] The first centered on religious liberty—a gift to the U.S. bishops who were in a major tussle with the Obama administration over the requirements of the Affordable Care Act. The second focused on climate change, where he found the Obama administration to be a comfortable ally.

The event was a success, echoed by the crowd's applause as the pope's speech was relayed on jumbotrons throughout the National Mall. Afterward, as the guests filed out, some of us retired into the White House for the private meetings. The pope and the president met by themselves while another group of us—the vice president, the secretary of state, and others—convened with Cardinal Parolin and his four-person delegation.

It was the vice president who opened the discussion asking about the Cuban visit and finally, Venezuela. The discussion could have gone on for many more hours, but the pope was now headed to a nearby Catholic Charities center followed by the rest of his program for the day.

1   President Barack Obama and his
    delegation enter the Apostolic Palace
    to meet with Pope Francis,
    March 27, 2014.

2   Pope Francis meeting Ambassador Hackett
    and his wife, Joan, with President Barack
    Obama at the White House,
    September 23, 2015.

Pope Francis departing Joint Base 3
Andrews in the Fiat Cinque Cento,
September 22, 2015.

Pope Francis addresses U.S. Congress 4
with Vice President Joe Biden and
Speaker John Boehner seated behind,
September 25, 2015.

5 The opening of the new United
States Embassy in Italy,
September 9, 2015.

❖ ⚜ ❖

6 Pope Francis greets U.S. Vice President
Joe Biden after delivering remarks on cancer
at the Vatican's International Conference on
Regenerative Medicine in Vatican City,
April 29, 2016.

Asantehene, Otumfuo Nana Osei 7
Tutu II seated on his throne
in Ghana, 2016.

Asantehene, Otumfuo Nana Osei Tutu II 8
and Ambassador Hackett at the
Acqua Santa Golf Course,
September 5, 2016.

7

THE POPE AT
THE CAPITOL

UPON LEARNING THAT the pope was to visit the United States, then Speaker of the House of Representatives John Boehner quickly invited the pope to address a joint session of Congress.[1]

Once we received the request, we knew that the event would be historic. I was handed the invitation, addressed to the pope, during a visit to Washington, and I duly delivered it to the Secretariat of State on my return to Rome.

Given the likelihood that the pope's visit would eventuate, I asked the speaker's staff to walk me through the space that the Holy Father would traverse while in the Capitol. The staff member was tentative but informative. Since the agenda had yet to be finalized, she led me through what she thought might be the schedule. I was concerned about the statue of Fr. Junipero Serra in the Capitol building. It was a point of minor controversy among some Native American groups, certainly not all, regarding the missionary strategies of past times. I thought that the pope, planning his canonization, ought not linger there. Protesters might use the monument as a rallying point. Entering the main chamber, I wondered how well the speech from this pope—

the first pope ever to address the Congress—would go. The galleries above, under which are portraits of lawmakers, including two popes, surround the hall. This august place would be packed with listeners. What message would Pope Francis bring?

Once the itinerary for the papal trip had been announced, the next step for the embassy was to identify expectations and figure out how to deal with them. The Vatican knew what it wanted: the Latin American pope visible in the United States sending a message of faith to American Catholics by word and example. But now, the trip had expanded to include stops at the White House and Congress in Washington, D.C., and ground zero at the site of the World Trade Center and the United Nations in New York City. Equally, there were the pastoral elements, including the National Basilica in Washington for the canonization of Fr. Junipero Serra, the Mass in Madison Square Garden, and the World Meeting of Families event in Philadelphia. Trying to assist the various U.S. entities with their expectation levels was the challenge.

From my side, Congress was to be the most challenging but offered the greatest opportunity. Joint sessions of Congress are rare, and people pay attention to them. Entire speeches are often broadcast on C-SPAN; this one would be broadcast on CNN and elsewhere. Parts of it are dissected, with the media analysts parsing every phrase. To the extent possible, I tried to communicate to the Vatican speechwriters the analysis they could expect from the Washington media. This was not the first papal visit, but it was a first to a Joint Session of Congress and it was Pope Francis, who had become like a rock star. Francis's message to Congress was, like himself, humble and honest. Whatever the pundits might spin, it was hard to misinterpret his meaning.

As the day and time for the pope's arrival at the Congress approached, I found myself seated in the balcony near Muriel Bowser, the mayor of the District of Columbia, and a few other friends. From this perch we were able to see most of the members of Congress, the justices of the Supreme Court, and the joint chiefs of staff. There was also a viewing area set up on a terrace outside the Capitol where a larger number was able to view Pope Francis's speech. The sergeant at arms brought us all to attention with his announcement: "Mr. Speaker, the pope of the Holy See." The pope's entrance commanded a standing ovation and lengthy applause. His opening sentence set the tone: "I am most grateful for your invitation to address this Joint Session of Congress in the 'land of the free and the home of the brave,'" generating, again, a hearty and lengthy standing applause. The audience was excited about his being there and especially that he was quoting well-known phrases about American life.[2]

Pope Francis went on to identify the special responsibility that being a member of Congress entails. He stated, "Your own responsibility as members of Congress is to enable this country, by your legislative activity, to grow as a nation. You are the face of its people, their representatives. You are called to defend and preserve the dignity of your fellow citizens in the tireless and demanding pursuit of the common good."

He continued speaking about the political history of the country, but cautioned, however, that "if politics must be truly at the service of the human person, it follows that it cannot be a slave to the economy or finance."

He then went on to identify and trace the achievements of four great Americans. First, Abraham Lincoln, followed by Martin Luther King, Dorothy Day, and Thomas Merton. He wove them into a matrix of concerns about violent conflict, hatred, and brutal atrocities, immigration, and social activism. The "passion for justice and the cause of the oppressed" were addressed, referencing Dorothy Day. She was a journalist, social activist, and best known as a Catholic pacifist and founder of the Catholic Worker Movement in New York City. "Care for creation" was outlined in the example of Thomas Merton, a Trappist monk, mystic, and author of *The Seven Storey Mountain*—one of the most influential pieces of religious literature about a man's search for faith and peace. I knew where this came from! It was a conjunction of the two books that I had recommended to the most probable papal speech writer: Paul Elie's *The Life You Save May Be Your Own* and David Brooks's book *The Road to Character*.

It was a moving speech, delivered well. With a bird's-eye perspective from the upper balcony of the chamber, I noticed that most stood and applauded on his arrival and at moments throughout his speech. There was a noticeable minority of Congressmen seated together who did not initially clap or stand. As the tenor of the presentation went on, they eventually sucked in their animus and rose with everybody else in the hall and applauded.

The place was electric. The moment charged everyone emotionally, and especially Speaker Boehner, for whom this event was to be his crowning achievement, as he was to resign a few weeks later.

The speech did what it was intended to do. It showed a pope who was ready to call people to action and to exhibit the responsibilities that they accepted in the office. It also showed the American people the substance of this pope. One of my staff commented that it made American Catholics feel good and proud of their faith.

We did not accompany, nor were we invited to the pope's next events at a Catholic Charities center in a church close to the Capitol. The separation of church and state filtered through the various events. Even though I had worked with CRS for forty years, as ambassador, I was wearing a different hat. We gratefully accepted every invitation that was extended to us by the Church.

Basilica of the National Shrine of the Immaculate Conception

The next day, bright and early, we set out for our reserved seats at the Basilica of the National Shrine of the Immaculate Conception on the campus of the Catholic University of America on Massachusetts Avenue. The crowds were enormous. This was to be the moment when the pope would canonize Fr. Junipero Serra, the intrepid and somewhat controversial Franciscan who spread the Catholic Church's teachings throughout California.

Washington's Hispanic families were present in sizable numbers but so were other well-known Washington Catholics and other Catholics who wanted to be seen. Two rows ahead of us was my predecessor, Secretary Jim Nicholson. He was seated close to the then presidential candidate Jeb Bush, who was forced during most of the

ceremony to greet campaign well-wishers, much to the obvious chagrin of his wife seated alongside him. Several justices of the Supreme
Court, including John Roberts, were in attendance. The campus
grounds were packed and overflowing.

Ensconced in our seats, Antoinette Hurtado, our public diplomacy officer, Peter Martin, Joan, and I, marveled at the enormous,
well-organized crowd. When the Mass ended, however, we realized
that the plan for exiting had fallen apart. We all started moving to the
driveway at the front of the basilica. We were then told to turn around
and find another exit. This meant thousands of people were pressing
against each other in opposite directions. We seemed to circle around
the same groups of buildings. It took us a while, but I had the chance
to bump into many friends, ex-CRS staff and acquaintances, as we
worked our way down a narrow driveway. Somehow, we found an exit
and rushed back to the hotel to grab our luggage. We were on the next
stop of this event-filled trip.

The Big Apple and the City of Brotherly Love

Following the Mass at the basilica, Antoinette, Peter, Joan, and I
raced to Union Station to catch a train to New York City. The pope's
transport would precede us there, especially since American Airlines
was shuttling him to JFK Airport on a plane duly decaled with his
papal insignia. There, U.S. Marine Corps helicopters brought him
into the city. Knowing the hectic schedule, unfortunately, we would
miss his interfaith prayer service at ground zero. We arrived at Penn
Station late at night. Finding our hotel, we readied for another important event, Pope Francis's address to the General Assembly of the
United Nations.

The United Nations

Early the next morning, we headed over to the U.S. Mission to
the United Nations located on First Avenue. It was walking distance

from our hotel, but as security was tight around the United Nations, I made extra sure we set out early and had all our identification and badges visible.

The official U.S. delegation was to be led by our then U.S. ambassador to the United Nations, Samantha Power, and included Ambassador Rose Gottemoeller, the under secretary of state for arms control and international security at the time, Senator Ed Markey of Massachusetts, Congressman Dan Kildee of Michigan, and myself. Ambassador Power's deputy, Ambassador Michele Sison, also accompanied us. The pope's address was expected to emphasize peace, combatting poverty, and climate change. Our delegation certainly represented people whose life's work and careers exemplified those sentiments.

I previously had extensive dealings with Senator Markey, my classmate in the class of 1968 at Boston College. On several occasions, while I was president of CRS, I testified in Congress on matters concerning food programs, environmental degradation, and health initiatives. In turn, Senator Markey had come to the Vatican on my watch to discuss various aspects of climate and the environment prior to the Paris Agreement, the international treaty on climate change often referred to as the Paris Accords or the Paris Climate Accords. Joan and I hosted him for a luncheon at the Residence in Rome, and I accompanied him to various meetings at the Vatican.

As noted earlier, under secretary Rose Gottemoeller came to the Vatican on two occasions during my tenure. I had invited her to speak to various individuals in the Secretariat of State and other offices on the issue of nuclear nonproliferation. I had served with her sister on the U.S. Conference of Catholic Bishops' Committee on International Justice and Peace. Rose went on to become the deputy secretary general of NATO in 2016.

Coincidentally, I first met Ambassador Sison some months before in December 2014, in Colombo, Sri Lanka, where she was serving as the U.S. ambassador. I traveled to Colombo at the invitation of Caritas Sri Lanka to speak at the tenth memorial of the tsunami that ravaged thousands of families in that country. She had now, only recently, taken up the post as deputy representative of the United States to the United Nations under Ambassador Power in New York City.

The pope planned to visit Sri Lanka in January 2015, shortly after my return from Colombo. While there, Ambassador Sison had given me an in-depth briefing on the political situation there. The country would hold a presidential election on January 8, five days before the papal visit. She indicated that the incumbent was already using the papal visit to his apparent advantage in the run up to the election. Furthermore, she posited potential violence if the incumbent lost the election. I came away feeling that the papal visit was ill-advised, even though it was to occur following the election.

When I returned from Colombo and met with individuals at the Vatican Secretariat of State, I expressed my view that the papal visit should at least be postponed. Of course, they had their own sources of information, and the Holy Father himself had his own views, for the Jesuits have a long tradition in the country. As well, Malcolm Cardinal Ranjith of Colombo, who served as the number two at Propaganda Fide and as apostolic nuncio in Jakarta, had an important influence on the visit.

I felt very much at home with this UN delegation. I had not yet met Congressman Kildee, though I came to learn that he represented Flint, Michigan, and was dogged in his attempts to obtain the release of Amir Mirza Hekmati, a constituent and former United States Marine, who traveled to Iran to visit a sick relative and was arrested and imprisoned for over four years for allegedly spying for the CIA in Iran.

As we filed into the General Assembly Hall, we learned that seating at the United Nations General Assembly of delegations was rotational; country delegations were seated in the front in one General Assembly; and at other times, the middle or the back. On this occasion, it just so happened that the U.S. delegation was seated in the front, just to the left of the speaker's podium. Thus, we were up very close to hear the pope's inspirational call for peace and environmental justice.

Some interpreted the speech as a rebuke of world leaders and governments for not doing enough in the pursuit of peace, the care for the migrants and refugees, and the care for the environment. I viewed it more as an inspirational and powerful call to action.

As we exited, I was directed by Antoinette Hurtado to an interview with Christiane Amanpour just outside the United Nations at Forty-Eighth Street and First Avenue. There were a host of other press setup on the sidewalk. I had walked, ridden my bike, and taken the bus past this point for twelve years when I worked for CRS at its headquarters nearby on Fifty-Fifth and First. I lived thirty blocks south on Twentieth and First. During all those trips, I never imagined being interviewed here on the sidewalk. It just goes to show that anything can happen in New York City.

Madison Square Garden

That evening we made our way to Madison Square Garden for the papal Mass where, courtesy of New York's Cardinal Timothy Dolan, we were hosted in a private box flush with food before the Mass. Our partners in the box were a very cordial couple from New Jersey. He was Cardinal Dolan's dentist, and we were grateful to share this wonderful moment with them.

About fifteen minutes before the Mass began, we were told to find our seats. We had a good view of the altar and when the pope arrived, the Garden erupted with applause. The Popemobile circled the crowd, and the cheers were deafening. However, the most memorable part of the ceremony was Cardinal Tim Dolan's words of welcome following the Mass. In the classic "Tim Dolan style," it was big, warm, and gracious and the crowd went wild. You would have thought that the Knicks or the Rangers had won the championship or the Stanley Cup. Twenty thousand people almost blew the roof off.

Philadelphia

The next stop for us was a train to Philadelphia. We arrived at the 30th Street Amtrak train station around 10:00 p.m. to discover that twenty blocks east of the train station to Center City, and north and south for about ten blocks were closed to traffic. The National Guard was visible with flood lights on almost every other block and large barriers were being constructed to block certain streets. Fences were erected on sidewalks to contain pedestrians. No taxis were allowed inside this zone.

So off we walked, in the dark of night on the eerily empty eighteen-plus blocks, to our hotel, pulling our suitcases and wishing the wheels were a bit larger.

The next day, we met our daughter and son—Jenny and Michael—who arrived from Baltimore. The venue for the 10:30 a.m. Mass was a small basilica; only 1,600 seats were available to the public. We did not have tickets as they were in short supply. Anyway, they were best used for individuals and friends of the Archdiocese of Philadelphia who rarely have the chance to attend a papal Mass. But we did all go to Independence Mall, also on foot from the hotel. It was a stunning backdrop as the pope spoke in front of the hall, the home of the Liberty Bell. He was welcomed on this stage by Sally Jewell, the secretary for the interior, and Mayor Michael Nutter. As with all previous venues, the anticipation was mounting high and the pope's message on immigration and religious freedom was poignant.

We watched the evening musical program on TV. It was quite the event with the likes of Aretha Franklin, Andrea Bocelli, the Colombian rock star Juanes, and the Philadelphia Orchestra. The atmosphere was truly festive.

On Sunday, we followed the thousands who walked to the Benjamin Franklin Parkway, the venue for the World Meeting of Families Mass and the closing celebrations. Jim Crowley, a friend of ours from Amelia Island, met us at our hotel. He knew his way around Philadelphia, where he grew up, as well as around the halls of the Vatican, where he assisted Bishop Vincenzo Paglia, the head of the Pontifical Council on the Family. Jim pointed out all the landmarks on our walk of a mile or so. We passed the Catholic Church of Sts. Peter and Paul, which displayed hundreds of rope knots. Attentive to a devotion the pope developed after studies in Germany, this church encouraged visitors to add or remove knots in its outside grotto as symbols of prayer requests and answers. The pope later passed by the grotto and blessed it before departing the city.

We were lucky to find extra tickets and met my brother, Bud, and his daughter, Cara, who drove from Bethlehem, Pennsylvania. Cara, a student at Temple University, was volunteering with the mayor's office in Philly and knew her way around the city well.

The crowds were enormous. The outdoor venue included part of a main thoroughfare and park and the stairway to the Philadelphia Museum of Art, made famous by the *Rocky* movies. Some estimates indicated that the numbers may have reached one million.

The audience was moved when the pope spoke of holiness in small gestures—quiet things done by mothers and grandmothers, fathers and grandfathers, siblings, signs of tenderness and compassion. I noticed many around me welling up and dabbing tears from their eyes.

There were many who were led to the altar for his blessing. A young man suffering from cerebral palsy approached the pope in a wheelchair. There was a family from Syria, who we at the embassy had helped get visas to the United States upon the request of Bishop Paglia, and many others.

The pope's time in Philadelphia also included a notable visit on Sunday to the Curran-Fromhold Correctional Facility for a meeting with a dozen hardcore prisoners, and a visit to St. Joseph's University, a Jesuit university on the outskirts of the city. Overall, he left with a very positive impression of Philadelphia and the United States.

I had to leave my wife and family toward the end of the Mass to board a van that would take me to an airport hall where the Holy Father would greet groups to offer final goodbyes. These were mostly "heavy hitters" and contributors to the Archdiocese of Philadelphia. The Secret Service told me where to stand. I wasn't there to get the "handshake," but rather to be in line with those at the plane to wish him goodbye. It took some convincing the Secret Service to make my way through—without being shot or tackled—to get to the red carpet leading to the plane.

Along with Vice President Biden and his family, Archbishop Chaput, and the mayor, I was positioned to offer my goodbye. Most ambassadors accept a seat to ride home with the pope on a plane that the host country offers. I, however, relinquished that place as I wanted to spend a few days with my family. We all bid farewell to the American Airlines flight carrying its Vatican guests back to the Eternal City.

Pope Francis's visit proved to be most successful and somewhat transformative. It was affirming to hear non-Catholic folks come to me and say, "I love your pope." For those many critics who did not like his informality, they were temporarily disarmed by his magnetism. For those who were oblivious to the pope, it was a wake-up moment. And for those who cared deeply about the issues of climate change, care for the marginalized, and those in poverty, they felt affirmed.

People—Catholics, non-Catholics, and even nonbelievers—were absolutely taken with him. His simple and direct way of speaking, his humility, and his charitable gestures touched people's hearts.

Some who had political agendas tried to find lows. This included some U.S. Catholic bishops. But for the vast majority, his visit was a beacon of sanity and amity, and many thought how our world would constructively be if we followed his advice.

8

THE NEW
CHANCERY
BUILDING

TOWARD THE END of our orientation for ambassadors in July 2013, John Petit, the administrative support individual for U.S. missions to the Vatican, Italy, France, Spain, and Portugal, took me to the Office of Overseas Building Operations (OBO). As I later learned, OBO is an autonomous entity, located across the river in Arlington, Virginia. It is autonomous because if every ambassador were to inject themselves into the process of building an embassy, there would be chaos.

OBO invited me to talk about the construction of a new embassy building and, more importantly, a move from the current location on the Aventine Hill overlooking the Circus Maximus (Circo Massimo). The new location was to be on the same compound/campus that was home to the United States Embassy to Italy and the United States Mission to the United Nations.[1] The building was the former headquarters of an Italian insurance company built in 1927. By 2013, half of the building was in a state of disuse. The other half housed various back-office functions for the U.S. Tri-mission Italy, such as the medical unit, the IT department, the agricultural attaché to Italy, and the like.[2]

As I entered the OBO meeting room, I sensed a significant hesitation as though there was a presumption that I was aware of the controversy that surrounded the decision to relocate the Embassy of the United States to the Holy See. I was not. (I had not yet had my luncheon with former Ambassador Nicholson). There was almost an expectation that I was going to take a negative view of the move and reverse it, something that I could have done. Although I didn't appreciate fully why my predecessors had refused to support a move, I understood the need for security and the economic saving that prompted this relocation.

In 2007, I had moved the 350 staff of Catholic Relief Services in Baltimore to a new location in the city, where we had more space and received a LEED Gold rating after construction was completed.[3] There were challenges and complaints: "What do you mean by no private offices?" "Who chose that salmon color?" I wasn't fearful of the challenge of moving chanceries. More space, less cost, and greater safety seemed a no-brainer. I was, however, still ignorant of the controversies surrounding the move. Soon, I began to learn the tenor and the temperature of the debate.

A week or so later, I had lunch with Secretary Jim Nicholson, who served as the United States ambassador to the Holy See under President George W. Bush and as his secretary of veteran's affairs following his time as ambassador. It was not long into the lunch at the Metropolitan Club that he raised the issue of the relocation of the embassy. He virulently opposed it. His grounds for opposition were, first, that we would find ourselves subsumed under "mother Italy" (U.S. Embassy to Italy); and second, that the Vatican did not want, nor would they approve, two embassies—the embassy to Italy and the one to the Holy See—located in the same building; and third, that it was an attempt by President Obama to downgrade the relationship between the United States and the Holy See.

The proposal to move the embassy had been previously raised by OBO with Ambassadors Nicholson and Rooney, both of whom had blocked it. I do not know whether the matter of the move was presented to Ambassadors Glendon and Diaz.

By this time, the world was just beginning to understand the power of the personality that is Pope Francis. It was also a world wherein the attack on the consulate in Benghazi, Libya, was still on people's minds. For me, the colocation matter was less of a concern because the compound was several blocks long and wide. It even had a small street inside it. The new embassy would be in a separate building, and it would face a street called Via Sallustiana and not Via Veneto, the street where the U.S. Embassy to Italy was located. Regarding Ambassador Nicholson's first objection, I had no history and no other input. I could only imagine what it might be like if the ambassador to Italy tried to encroach on Embassy Vatican purview. Before my time, there was an instance of a previous U.S. ambassador to Italy who bypassed Vatican protocol by going around Embassy Vatican to get a handshake with Pope Benedict XVI, much to the chagrin of our embassy and curial staff responsible for such arrangements. He used his Italian connections with the *gentiluomini*, the famous pontifical ushers. The situation was tantamount to the ambassador of the United States to France arranging to meet the queen of England without consulting the U.S. ambassador to Great Britain. Ambassadors are supposed to stay in their lane. I had no indication that this was going to happen, and I often took time to educate and explain that Vatican City was the address of a separate, stand-alone, sovereign country, which would not stand for a break in protocol.

On the third issue, I smelled the politics and understood the ongoing debates between the Obama administration and the U.S. bishops on health care and religious liberty; the relocation was a way to add more fuel to the fire.

When I got to Rome, I quickly realized that, while my office had a beautiful view of the Circo Massimo, it was much too close to the street and far too insecure—the distance from the sidewalk below to my office window was less than a throw from a pitcher's mound. As an office, the entire chancery building was cramped and dysfunctional—the second-floor roof was slanted so that anyone above five-and-a-half feet had to bend to get to their desks.

Additionally, the rent was exorbitant. To be certain, the embassy had a history on the Aventine that former ambassadors appreciated, and, of course, there was political posturing. But the times of safety and economy had changed, and a move was inevitable. It was, however, a great place for staff to watch the Mick Jagger concert that took place at the Circo Massimo in 2015. Staff were very pleased when I let them use the yard at the chancery for a barbecue on the night of the concert.

We arrived in Rome in September, and I presented our credentials the next month. On November 25, my journal entry noted that the issue of the "embassy move spurred by Jim Nicholson has become nettlesome." Nicholson had gained allies in former Ambassadors Ray Flynn, Thomas Melady, Mary Ann Glendon, and Francis Rooney.

Ireland, which had a similar controversy in closing their embassy to the Holy See, saw a headline appear in the Irish press that stated, "Obama Administration Plans to Close Vatican Embassy, Shock Move." Barbie Latza Nadeau, correspondent-at-large for the *Daily Beast*, wrote something equally inane. The headline read, "U.S. Pulls Embassy out of the Vatican." There are no embassies inside Vatican City and there haven't been since the Second World War, when a few ambassadors worked from inside the walls of the Vatican. But I learned many years ago that stupidity abounds, and that common sense often becomes an uncommon commodity.

When presidential candidate Jeb Bush made a statement criticizing the Obama administration for closing the Embassy to the Holy See, I realized ignorance (or fake news) to promote malintent was overflowing. He tweeted, "Why would our President close our Embassy to the Vatican? Hopefully, it is not retribution for Catholic organizations opposing Obamacare."[4] I thought, *Doesn't Jeb have any staff?* He was not alone; many journalists failed to do the minimum research. The U.S. Embassy to the Holy See was never located in the Vatican, and it was not closing.

Growing up in the West Roxbury section of Boston, a fight was something one learned how to manage. This proposal, which I approved, was developing into a real clash.

I now knew that the decision to move was the correct one. The plans depicted a grand structure with ample space, elegance, functionality, security, cost savings, and independence. It was an unused section of a much larger building, constructed in Italy's heyday of the early twentieth century, when no expense was spared. It had an elegant marble staircase. In one of the offices on the first floor hung a seventy-foot mural by the Italian artist Afro Basaldella, whose works are shown in the Guggenheim Museum in New York City. All around were the trappings of the elegance of the 1920s.

Opposition to the move was used more as a talking point and to make a case that President Obama had a problem with the Vatican. More precisely, some opponents of President Obama wanted to construct a problem with the Vatican. It was all political!

There was, however, a strong case made by Ambassador James Creagen, who stressed what he perceived as the potential for the U.S. Embassy to Italy to usurp the Vatican agenda. His information dated back to when he served as deputy chief of mission at the Embassy to the Holy See under President Clinton. Those days had passed. That was early enough in the history of the embassy and under an administration that had only a mild appreciation of the reach and influence of the Holy See. At that time, there may have been an existential threat to Embassy Vatican's survival. He made a principled case for what life at the U.S. Embassy to the Holy See was in the 1980s. But that was then; and this is now.

Given the heightened concerns for security within the department and the terribly high (outrageous) rental cost for the Aventine building, it was crystal clear to me that we should move. Except for the politics, the fact that we would have a larger, more appropriate structure was an obvious slam dunk. All the appropriate parties at the Vatican were advised in advance and understood the benefits of the move. They wanted some assurance that we would have our own access, signage, and be visibly distinct from the Embassy to Italy. These things we promised and delivered. In fact, the new chancery is separate from the chancery building of the U.S. Embassy to Italy. Though the two buildings are near to each other, they face out to different streets and have different addresses.

The controversy burned from the moment I got there until the renovation of the building was completed in August 2015. Two congressional delegations came to Rome and wanted to see the "downgraded" embassy. Additionally, we had two visits from Speaker Boehner's staff, as he was being pressured to investigate and possibly withhold funding for the renovations.

All this disappeared with an on-site appreciation that this was going to be a much grander, more functional chancery with our own "Sensitive Compartmented Information Facility" (SCIF), which the old embassy could not accommodate. The new chancery had character and was an appropriate representation of our country and our recognition of the importance of our relations with the Holy See. Despite this, some refused to accept what they saw because it didn't fit into their political perceptions.

Though perhaps not my biggest challenge, this relocation of the embassy was mostly political and had to be managed.

One other important area of management was Italy's summer *ferragosto*, roughly translated "gone fishing, it's August." The entire nation shuts down because it is very hot, but not any worse than Washington, D.C., or Baltimore in the summer. Fortunately for me, Pope Francis announced that he would take no vacation other than a spiritual retreat for two weeks. He requested that the traditional papal summer home be opened to the public. Thus, Castel Gandolfo, a hillside villa with gorgeous gardens, an ancient Roman amphitheatre, and ruins, became a museum open to the world. All this allowed me to insist on the continuation of the construction of the new embassy throughout the summer. I chose to stay in Italy, taking small trips on weekends, and as a result, I was always around asking for and receiving regular updates on the construction. The embassy was completed on time and on budget, which some consider a miracle.

Upon completion—maybe even before the paint was dry—I showed the head of the Vatican protocol office around the new building, and he was duly impressed.

The official opening of the embassy was a grand affair with representation from the Secretariat of State along with diplomats from virtually all other embassies to the Holy See. The presence of the Vatican's gendarmerie band added flare as they played both the national anthem of the Vatican as well as that of the United States, "The Star-Spangled Banner."

This all occurred in a ground-floor atrium surrounded by statues, remaining from National Insurance Institute (ANI). Entering the heavy entrance door and security booth, visitors are greeted to a massive, winding marble stairway, beautifully appointed with ceiling windows and statues. Everything in the embassy was restored according to the original look as seen in pictures, using stored furniture and paintings. Even the ambassador's office wallpaper (in fact, cloth) was matched from remnants. The strong symbols of bundled grains and workman's tools are imbedded and engraved in cornices and wooden wall covering, all harking back to the fascist era before it turned extreme. The Office of Building Operations, their contractors, and the art/historical staff at the Embassy Italy deserve enormous credit for preserving a historical monument of a grand Italian era as well as making the building functional again.

Other than perhaps the French and Spanish embassies to the Holy See, which have each accumulated treasures and masterpieces collected over centuries and are housed in old Roman stately grandeur, our new chancery stands as the finest in the diplomatic community to the Holy See.

9

THE MAKING OF
AN ENCYCLICAL

ENCYCLICALS ARE LETTERS from a pope circulated to bishops around the world as a statement or interpretation of Sacred Scripture or Tradition. They are not necessarily an infallible teaching of a pope, but they can be. Nevertheless, they are documents that require close attention if you are observing Catholic Church teaching.

Even as early as fall 2013, it was thought that Pope Francis might be thinking of issuing an encyclical on the environment. In fact, this idea had arisen under Pope Benedict XVI. But only those who were true insiders or those deeply enmeshed in the topic would understand that the Holy See was preparing something prior to the 2015 United Nations Climate Change Conference, COP 21, that was held in Paris, France, from November 30 to December 12, 2015.

The general population was waiting for some published statements to give insight as to what the new pope really thought. It was not long after his election in 2013 that Pope Francis issued his first apostolic exhortation, *Evangelii Gaudium* (The Joy of the Gospel).[1] It garnered far more interest from the diplomatic community than usual, more for its explanation of a thought process than its actual content. He laid out four principals that were read as fundamentals that guided his thinking. In addition, the clarity and simplicity of the prose made it readable by almost everyone. It was a teaching document—a "how-to" spread of the gospel.

Profound in its simplicity, it is a powerful document that covers much territory. It outlines the four principles for a peaceful society, seeming to add a practical edge as well as an ideology. The principles are the following:

- Time is greater than space.
- Unity prevails over conflict.
- Realities are more important than ideas.
- The whole is greater than the parts.[2]

The diplomatic community began to look for those principles in his remarks and writing, and indeed, they were there. This document indicated that this pope was moved by both strong theological and philosophical principles. For some, the document was disorienting, as it challenged certain lifestyle motivations. In fact, in his January 2019 address to the Diplomatic Corps, he annunciated these principles again.[3]

While some interpreted *Evangelii Gaudium* as anticapitalist, there were many more anxiously hopeful for what might be coming concerning a moral obligation to save the planet. Many people, both inside and outside the U.S. government, contacted us through 2014 and 2015, attempting to gain access to the process of developing the document on the environment; others wanted to lend their expertise. One of the first from the United States, as you might expect, was former Vice President Al Gore.[4] The Vatican was not ready or willing to engage with him on the issue, and his suggestion that he would like to meet with the pope was not entertained. Clearly, the Vatican did not want to appear to be influenced by any one country. They wished to speak globally from their own platform.

Being new on the job, and with the position of ambassador having been vacant from November 2012 until my arrival in September 2013, not even the embassy staff had any special insight or access regarding the encyclical's development.

By mid-2014, it was clear that a document was in the offing and that the Pontifical Council of Justice and Peace was the principal drafter. However, the Council staff were very tight-lipped on the matter and were not open to unsolicited suggestions. They very likely realized how fraught with controversy this document would be. The debate on climate change was swirling, fueled by big energy, big coal, and just plain folks who did not agree that changes in the climate were the result of human actions.

I do not know which specific individuals contributed to the science underpinning the development of this encyclical. I was familiar with some of those who had an active engagement with the Vatican in the past. There was a cast of scientists, conservationists, and climate activists, including Dr. Jeffrey Sachs, the current director of the Center for Sustainable Development and former director of the Earth Institute at Columbia University; Dr. Hans Joachim Schellnhuber, the founding director of the Potsdam Institute for Climate Impact Research; Dr. Naomi Oreskes, who became professor of the history of science and affiliated professor of earth and planetary sciences at Harvard University in 2013; Dr. Veerabhadran Ramanathan of the Scripps Institution of Oceanography at the University of California, San Diego; and others.

This group tends to attract controversy among the so-called climate change denial community. In April 2015, just prior to the release of the long-awaited encyclical, *Laudato Si'*, the Heartland Institute and Marc Moreno held protests and a symposium at the Hotel Columbus located steps from St. Peter's Basilica. He chose to meet at a space on Via Della Conciliazione virtually beneath the windows of the Vatican, all with the hope of dissuading the pope from his agenda of a climate change action. By the time their protest took place, the encyclical had already been written, translated, and was probably at the publisher.

At the embassy, we had several visitors from the administration. Gina McCarthy, who was currently serving as the thirteenth administrator of the Environmental Protection Agency, came to support the Vatican's efforts to reduce the carbon footprint. We were able to arrange a meeting with Cardinal Peter Turkson, who was the president of the Pontifical Council for Justice and Peace, the department charged with issuing the encyclical. A lengthy discussion ensued where he and Administrator McCarthy found agreement on many climate issues. Interestingly, the Vatican also offered a tour of the power generation system in Vatican City as well as a behind-the-walls and ceiling visit to the Sistine Chapel. A new, state-of-the-art ventilation and heating project, contracted to the United States company United Technologies Carrier, and lighting systems designed by the German company Osram had recently been installed. We learned how the chapel's air and temperature were filtered and regulated to best preserve the art. Our group was then brought down to the bowels of the Vatican City's basement. Opened with a key, literally the size of your arm, we entered the cellars where the old diesel generator was decommissioned but still ready as a backup to the newer, and much more efficient, gas-operated power supply. The busts of several popes were displayed on pedestals even in the engine rooms. From there, we went to the dome of the basilica and outside, where we could view the solar panels situated on the Paul VI auditorium—another attempt by the Vatican to reduce its carbon footprint.

On two occasions, we had a visit from Senator Ed Markey, who has long been an activist on climate and ecological issues. We also arranged meetings for him with various Vatican officials. Like me, his training at Boston College had led him to the writings of the Jesuit priest Pierre Teilhard de Chardin, especially his *Hymn of the Universe*.[5] He was very animated about the necessity to couple the practical with the moral needs to address the climate crisis. At the time of his visit, it seemed almost certain that the encyclical would fulfill his hopes. In fact, the encyclical *Laudato Si'* was not borrowed from the French Jesuit philosopher, but rather from the simple writings of a medieval saint.[6]

The enthusiasm for this encyclical's release brought a wide range of individuals who wished to engage the Vatican on the issue. The embassy hosted several events, but we just could not accommodate the overwhelming interest and desire of people to meet at the top levels on this topic.

On May 24, 2015, the encyclical was announced, evoking both enthusiasm and consternation. Some excoriated the papal document as dabbling in science, but there could be no denying its main thesis: that all have the moral obligation to protect the earth. The timing was impeccable from our embassy's viewpoint. It was roughly three months before the pope's visit to the United States and well in advance of the United Nations Climate Change Conference in Paris, affording adequate time for debate. On June 18, 2015, the Vatican hosted a televised forum to promulgate the new encyclical.

This document was to become part of the stuff of his upcoming visit to the United States. Since the climate debate in the United States had taken on a political tone, we knew that it would be quite electric, but we also knew the positions of the Obama administration were in line with the encyclical.[7]

10

THE VATICAN

HAVING WORKED WITH the American bishops as well as bishops, clergy, and religious around the world, I knew well that being ambassador to the Holy See is not like being ambassador to any other country. The Vatican is, simply, not like any other country. It's not exactly a riddle wrapped in a mystery, but certainly an enigma. Considering that it is only a few square miles of real estate and some assorted buildings in and around Rome, it is counterintuitive but true to state that it engages and represents over a billion adherents around the world. All these faithful are citizens of other countries, and each of these states have their own ambassadors to the Holy See.

Thus, the ambassador is an envoy both to a physical place—the Sovereign State of the Holy See with actual people—and to an idea—a belief, a faith. The few hundred people who work in Vatican City have a worldwide constituency. This global influence belies the size of the Vatican's physical footprint.

The Vatican reaches its adherents through a global structure called a hierarchy—the cardinals, archbishops, and bishops. It also includes the clergy, religious communities of men and women, and the laity. But then there are various other instruments that carry the faith to the farthest reaches and outposts.

For the most part, I interacted daily with the various Vatican institutions that seemed, at times, to be somewhat byzantine or medieval. Pick your appropriate historical adjective. It could often be confusing, for its processes and procedures had evolved over decades and, in some instances, centuries. But no doubt my counterparts in more conventionally organized nations had their own sets of red tape to understand and manage.

I possessed a rudimentary knowledge of the inner workings of the curia before I took up my post as ambassador. During my time with Catholic Relief Services, if I was passing through Rome on my way back from a trip that I thought might be of interest to the Vatican, I would visit the appropriate office. I also served for several years on the Vatican guiding body for international Catholic charitable organizations, the Pontifical Council Cor Unum for Human and Christian Development.[1] And for six years, I also served as the North American vice president of Caritas Internationalis, the Rome-based umbrella body for Caritas/Catholic Charities in 167 countries. As one of four North American members of Caritas Internationalis, CRS often served on its governing board.

Consequently, I knew personalities and specific areas among the curial offices that related to my agendas at Catholic Relief Services, but I never got to see the larger picture of how offices worked together or sometimes independently.

The approach of an ambassador was to be significantly different. Our most direct, formal, and frequent contact was with the second section of the Secretariat of State. That office deals with governments and international organizations such as the United Nations and its agencies, as well as other intergovernmental bodies. Shortly after I arrived, Cardinal Pietro Parolin took over as secretary of state from Cardinal Tarcisio Bertone. Cardinal Parolin moved to the position from his post as apostolic nuncio in Caracas, Venezuela. Though his title was secretary of state, most would suggest that he served, in essence, as the Vatican's prime minister.

Interestingly, the second section is better known than the first section, which functions as the pope's internal back office and deals with internal Church matters such as the appointment and oversight of papal nuncios. It directly assists the pope in the running of the universal Church. The two sections, generally, work hand-in-glove. During my tenure, the head of the first section was Archbishop Giovanni Angelo Becciu.

Pope Francis, as one who had never worked in the Roman curia, introduced a new personality into the running of the Church. As we noted earlier, he fabricated a "domestic Cabinet," the C-9, composed of nine cardinals representing geographic regions and three important offices of the Holy See, the secretary of state, the secretary of the economy, and the governor of Vatican City State. Since it was initially formed, it has engaged a vast and fundamental range of topics.

They have investigated the authorities and functioning of all the main dicasteries and councils. They have suggested changes and covered topics ranging from the training of the Vatican diplomats to requiring specific adjustments to the Vatican constitution that effectively established a third section within the Secretariat of State. Its specific purpose is to manage the Vatican's diplomatic representation outside the Vatican, the apostolic nuncios.[2] The new section freed up the *sostituto*, or deputy, and allowed more flexibility and time to implement the pope's internal organizational decisions.

One of Pope Francis's personal priorities was the theological status of bishops' conferences and his hope to evolve ways of decentralizing more authority to those conferences, a debate that has been long-standing and arduous. Additionally, a priority that he laid at the feet of the C-9 very early was the matter of "clericalism," a view that ordained ministers should be viewed as "above" the nonordained members of the Church. For Francis, this was a virus within the Church that had to be changed.

New Structures

In 2014, the Holy Father established a completely new body at a significantly senior level, the Secretariat for the Economy.[3] This was led by the Australian cardinal George Pell. The new Secretariat demonstrated the priority Francis placed on financial transparency.

It initially received a broad mandate to look at the financial manage-ment, investments, and accountability of all Vatican offices. It was further buttressed by a new Council for the Economy headed by the German cardinal Reinhard Marx, giving it maximum authority. Despite this heft, it met with resistance.

According to many observers, the formation of both the Secre-tariat and the Council for the Economy was a good idea. It was a new perspective and took on many of the entrenched financial practices of the Vatican. However, carrying out its full mandate proved more difficult than envisioned.

It was from this review by the C-9 that in 2015, a third Secre-tariat was established for Communications. It was a restructuring that absorbed the offices of Vatican TV (CTV); publications, including the Vatican daily paper, *L'Osservatore Romano*; the Pontifical Council for Social Communications; Vatican Radio; the Vatican Press Office; the Vatican Photo Service; the Vatican Internet Service; and the Vatican Printing Press into one.

Though it is the largest office in the Vatican, the influence of the Secretariat of Communications paled in comparison to the Secretariat of State. The same was true of the Secretariat of the Economy.

The Congregations

In the official organization chart under the three Secretariats were the Congregations, Dicasteries, Tribunals, Councils, and offices. Principal among the Congregations is the Doctrine of the Faith (the Holy Office), established in the mid-fifteenth century. Historically, it is the body most well known for carrying out the Inquisition. We had little to no dealing with this office, and many agreed that its influence has waned significantly in recent years. Its present-day mandate deals with promoting and safeguarding doctrine.

The Cardinal Prefect of the Congregation for the Oriental Churches is presided over by Cardinal Leonardo Sandri. This Con-gregation covers Vatican relations with the Eastern Rite churches throughout the world. While that might seem like a somewhat arcane area for our embassy's involvement, many of the Eastern churches are operating in the Middle East. Consequently, the embassy found itself interacting frequently with this Congregation. The staff in this office were a trove of both historical and current information about Egypt, India, Iraq, Lebanon, Syria, and elsewhere.

A most important office is "Prop," the colloquial name for Congregation for the Evangelization of Peoples,[4] whose influence is often overlooked and certainly understated. In operational terms, it ranked immediately below the Secretariat of State. Except for the Philippines and Australia, the Prop oversees the Church's activities in Africa, parts of the Americas, all of Asia, and Oceania, making it a powerful office with both influence over a fast-growing part of the universal Church and, equally important, the money to support its efforts. Churchgoers in the United States are familiar with the annual November collection for "missions." The same appeal is collected in every country in the world. That money goes to Prop, which was headed by the very experienced Cardinal Fernando Filoni. He had served as apostolic nuncio in Iraq throughout the early and bloodiest days of the Iraq war from 2001 to 2006. From 2007 to 2011, he served as the *sostituto* at the Secretariat of State, essentially the second highest official. More recently, Francis appointed Cardinal Tagle of the Philippines as its prefect.[5]

The embassy had frequent interaction with this office, although not as much as with the second section of the Secretariat of State. The staff in the Secretariat of State and the Congregations of Oriental Churches and Prop had far-reaching resources of information.

There are also many Congregations, such as the Congregation for Divine Worship and the Discipline of the Sacraments, the Congregation for the Causes of Saints, the Congregations for Bishops, for Clergy, for Institutes of Consecrated Life and Societies of Apostolic Life, and for Catholic Education, all of which had little to do with our mission.

Dicasteries

The Holy Father has established two new dicasteries, which are principal departments of the Roman curia. There are currently three dicasteries: the Dicastery for Communications; the Dicastery for the Laity, Family and Life, which is headed by Cardinal Kevin Farrell, an Irish American who served as the seventh bishop of Dallas; and the most recent one, the Dicastery for Promoting Integral Human Development, which focuses on a wide range of topics, including refugees and migrants, subsuming the work of what was formerly known as the Pontifical Council for Migrants and Itinerants.[6]

By combining various offices and creating new ones, the pope was removing the entrenched systems and giving them greater relevance.

The first prefect of the Dicastery for Promoting Integral Human Development was Cardinal Peter Turkson, who previously directed the Pontifical Council for Justice and Peace.

Our staff and I met regularly with the cardinal and members of his team on matters ranging from nuclear nonproliferation to the launch of *Laudato Si'* and positions the Holy See might take on certain treaties. I knew him from when he was the archbishop of Cape Coast in Ghana before he was moved to the Vatican.

Tribunals and Councils

Next in the structure of the Vatican are the tribunals, which engage in what for many seem to be the somewhat arcane but very necessary internal work of adjudication and legislation.

Considerable external engagement did take place within the Pontifical Councils, starting with the Pontifical Council for the Promotion of Christian Unity. Engagement with other Christian groups was its bread and butter. Our mission interacted with them regularly on Orthodox religions in Russia, Ukraine, and the Middle East, and they helped us understand much of the context of the meeting between Pope Francis and Patriarch Kirill in Cuba, as well as the aggression by Russia in the Ukraine.

While the Pontifical Council for Legislative Texts received none of our time, the Pontifical Council for Interreligious Dialogue was often in communication with us. They held ongoing dialogue with Islam, Buddhism, Hinduism, and other non-Christian religions. It was headed by the very talented and capable, if somewhat ailing, Cardinal Jean-Louis Tauran. Impaired by what appeared to be Parkinson's disease and terrible arthritis, he would not let up on his travels, though he clearly struggled. He was also one of the most frequent visitors to the Secretariat of State, where he had spent an important segment of his career. A wise and brilliant man, he shared many insights with me and my staff. He also held the title as the *camerlengo*, the individual who steps in during the period known as the *sede vacante* (empty seat) upon the death of a pope. More recently, this role (made famous by Dan Brown's *The DaVinci Code*), was assigned to then Msgr. Kevin Farrell.

We were particularly interested in the Pontifical Council for Interreligious Dialogue and their engagement with Islam. There were many aspects of the State Department that took a policy interest in this topic and developments that the Holy See was making in its relations with the more moderate trends of Islamic thinking. The pope invited Ahmed Mohamed Ahmed El-Tayeb, the Grand Imam (or Sheikh) of al-Azhar and former president of al-Azhar University—one of the most prestigious Sunni religious centers of learning—to the Vatican for dialogue. He then signed an important agreement with him during the pope's visit to Abu Dhabi. Then, during a trip to Morocco shortly after signing this agreement, the pope signed an agreement with 160 countries affirming that migration was a natural phenomenon and one that nations had to deal with benevolently.

The same policy alignment with the United States could be seen in the Council's work with Hinduism and Buddhism, especially regarding specific countries.

For some reason unknown to me, the Church's relations with Judaism fell within the ambit of the Pontifical Council for the Promotion of Christian Unity following Pope Paul VI's declaration *Nostra Aetate*. In fact, I recall meeting Fr. Nobert Hofmann of that Council in a cafe on Via Della Conciliazione on the morning when the fiftieth anniversary updated document of *Nostra Aetate* was issued. Obviously, I paid for his coffee.

Since American Jewish groups were regular visitors to the Vatican and often asked for our intervention, we met regularly with this Council. One memorable visit that occurred shortly after the release of the fiftieth anniversary of *Nostra Aetate* was from Rabbi Arthur Schneier of the Park East Synagogue in New York City and the Appeal of Conscience Foundation. He was well known in the Vatican, and people knew and respected him.

The Pontifical Council for Culture undertook some far-reaching and thought-provoking initiatives.[7] Its Courtyard of the Gentiles was a worldwide dialogue program that engaged those of non-Christian beliefs. They also led discussions on some of the provocative issues of our day such as ethical issues regarding bioscience. It was this Council that sponsored a conference on breakthroughs in regenerative medicine at which Vice President Biden spoke.

There are dozens of other offices that support the work of the pope. In addition, there are the Pontifical Academies, the Vatican Museum and Archives, and the Pontifical Universities run by religious communities.

The government organization is complex. Given the worldwide scope of the Catholic Church, it is a very streamlined and economical structure. Its staff works overtime with dedication, and the structure is an umbrella over all the far-reaching dioceses around the globe.

The Pontifical Academy of Sciences

One of the more interesting offices in Vatican City is the Pontifical Academy of Sciences, a branch of the Vatican that serves as a "think tank."

Pope Francis's concern regarding migrants and refugees was evident from the beginning of his papacy with his visit to Lampedusa, which became the first stop for refugees arriving from Libya. As we noted earlier, he also made clear another important issue for him when he sent a note to Bishop Marcelo Sanchez Sorondo, the Chancellor of the Pontifical Academy of Sciences and the Pontifical Academy of Social Sciences, regarding a report on human trafficking, stating in his tiny script, "Marcelo, what are we doing about this?"

In addition to being an issue for me, it was an issue already on the U.S. government's agenda. The Department of State has given this matter of human trafficking "policy focus" for over twenty years and, in 2001, issued its first annual Trafficking in Persons Report. It contains a rating of nations on three tiers as to their attaining minimal acceptable standards to eliminate human trafficking.

In the 1980s in the Philippines, when I served with Catholic Relief Services, we supported Caritas Manila's efforts against child prostitution and human trafficking. Religious sisters dressed in street clothes would go to the red-light areas of Manila and other cities to "rescue" young women, some younger than twelve years old, who had been forced into prostitution. CRS also worked on the issue in other parts of the world, for example, supporting "safe houses" in Beirut for women who had escaped servitude and abuse at the hands of their "employers," who too often were better described as "owners."

Following the Haiti earthquake in 2010, there were numerous reports of children being stolen or given away. When parents felt they were unable to raise their children because of poverty or other reasons, they placed them with other families or in so-called orphanages, some of which were questionable in character. There is an equally horrible practice of poor families in the mountains in Haiti who cannot afford school fees or even enough food: They send their children to live with a relative or friend in the cities. As *restaveks*, these children are subjected to terrible treatment and function more as slaves.

Too often in the chaos after the earthquake, these young children ended up across the border in the Dominican Republic, taken there by those who intended to sell them into sexual slavery or some other form of indentured existence. At CRS, we supported a community of religious sisters who set up a safe house at the border crossing with the Dominican Republic. They trained volunteers to patrol the border crossings surreptitiously and to identify anomalous situations involving young children whom they would bring to the attention of the police. In other instances, the police would turn the children over to the sisters, who would keep them secure until they could be safely returned to their families or relatives. Many children were saved.

It was encouraging that the charge by Pope Francis to Chancellor Sorondo was picked up with deliberateness and enthusiasm.

In November 2013, the Pontifical Academies held a meeting in conjunction with the World Federation of Catholic Medical Associations "to establish the real status quo and an agenda to combat this heinous crime. For example, natural sciences today can provide new tools that can be used against this new form of slavery, such as a digital registry to compare the DNA of unidentified missing children (including cases of illegal adoption) with that of their family members who have reported their disappearance."[8]

The following year, the Pontifical Academies held another meeting entitled "Young People against Prostitution and Human Trafficking," where it convened youth leaders and others to address this complex problem through empowerment, awareness raising, and the training, development, and strengthening of young people's networks. The basic goal was to empower young people to play a leading role within both governments and civil society "to change the paradigm and imagine a world without violence and prostitution, free of human trafficking."[9]

And in July 2015, shortly after the release of the pope's encyclical *Laudato Si'*, the Academy commissioned a symposium entitled "Social Exclusion and Climate Change." Mayors from around the world were invited to exchange ideas and thoughts about their engagements with these two perplexing and, at times, interconnected issues. For example, some mayors talked about the necessity of people to move because of droughts or loss of farmland, sending people into the cities where they can be easily exploited and trafficked into the sex trade; others offered examples of sustainable efforts to include growing populations of economically strapped people flooding into cities and living in squalid conditions.

The delegation for the United States consisted of California governor Jerry Brown, New York City mayor Bill DeBlasio, New Orleans mayor Mitch Landrieu, Boston mayor Marty Walsh, and a half-dozen others making a strong commitment to anti-trafficking.

Mayor Mitch Landrieu of New Orleans, for example, offered the harrowing tragedy of Hurricane Katrina. His experience in New Orleans was met with recognition and appreciation by mayors in other places around the globe that have experienced severe flooding or other climate-related events and have witnessed massive human displacement and increased vulnerability to human trafficking.

The Pontifical Academies lead very strong convening efforts around the topic of human trafficking and at the embassy; we were proud to contribute intellectual firepower in the personalities of Luis Cabeza de Baca, the former United States ambassador-at-large to Monitor and Combat Trafficking in Persons and his successor, Susan Coppedge.

The Australians, led by their ambassador to the Holy See, John McCarthy, were particularly taken with the issue they termed *human slavery*. But it got a bit muddled with the involvement of Andrew Forrest, an Australian businessman in the mining industry and philanthropist, who was listed as one of the top-ten richest Australians. In 2013, Forrest and his wife, Nicola, were the first Australians to pledge most of their wealth to charity.

At first, all seemed fine. Forrest was most encouraging to Ambassador McCarthy and offered to finance an office in Rome to work with the Vatican on a new nongovernmental initiative, the Global Freedom Network.[10]

The United Nations was preparing to release an updated set of sustainable development goals, and the Australians, along with many others, hoped that they would explicitly list human trafficking as one of the primary areas that needed attention. This would have also meant that there would be significant UN funds allocated to the human trafficking agenda.

Everything progressed well for the first year of the Global Freedom Networks' evolution. With Forrest's financing, the organization started to insert itself deeply and directly into the Vatican's human trafficking policy agenda. As recounted to me by Bishop Marcelo Sánchez Sorondo, Forrest wanted to use the leverage of the Holy See to influence the decision by the United Nations to make human trafficking one of its revised sustainable goals. If human trafficking were accepted as one of the goals, Forrest could claim credit. Bishop Sorondo, while agreeing that elevating the issue of human trafficking on the United Nation's agenda was noble, he and others did not want the Vatican used or "instrumentalized"—the term used in Vatican City.

Forrest gave money to the archbishop of Canterbury's representative based in Rome, Archbishop Sir David Moxon, to support his engagement on the issue. He also proposed supporting the work of the Vatican through the Pontifical Academy of Social Sciences. This is when the tension began.

Bishop Marcelo Sánchez Sorondo sensed that, while he held the position as chair of the board of directors for the Global Freedom Network, Mr. Forrest basically wanted to use his purchased access to the Vatican to dictate the agenda. A board room tussle ensued with an outcome that the Pontifical Academy on behalf of the Holy See distanced itself from work of the Global Freedom Network.

Bishop Sorondo told me that when he briefed the pope about the actions of Forrest and the happenings of the board of the Global Freedom Network, the pope's response was clear and direct: "Stay away from the money."

Nevertheless, ending its relationship with the Global Freedom Network did not end the Holy See's engagement with the issue. The Pontifical Academy of Social Sciences (PASS) along with other Vatican offices continued to hold meetings and symposia on the topic of human trafficking, convening various academicians and practitioners to share experiences and develop best practices.

Senator Bernie Sanders

The Pontifical Academies operate with a degree of autonomy and, therefore, were not always on the same page with other curial offices.

One such independent initiative of the Pontifical Academy was an invitation to Senator Bernie Sanders to attend a PASS meeting. It was on April 9, 2016, that I first heard that Senator Bernie Sanders was coming to the Vatican to attend the meeting and ultimately to meet the pope. We were amid the 2016 election campaign, and this would have been a major coup for Bernie's campaign. I considered this improper interference by the Holy See into our politics not unlike the Vatican's objections to use association with the pope to advance a cause. The debate about Russian hacking in our election seemed to overshadow the Sanders' visit, but it was nonetheless a dilemma facing the embassy.[11]

Upon learning of the Sanders visit, I immediately contacted the then under secretary for relations with states, Msgr. Antoine Camilleri—a position roughly equivalent to that of a deputy foreign minister—and told him in no uncertain terms that press publicity of the pope meeting Sanders should not happen. I explained that he must do something to block or cancel it, lest it look as though the Vatican was throwing its support behind Bernie. He was taken aback. He had not heard this was happening, and he promised to investigate it immediately. I counseled that at the very least he should not have a photo-op with Pope Francis.

I had nothing against Bernie. I thought some of his policy statements, albeit without backup plans, were good; but the principle here was wrong. This was a blatant attempt to "instrumentalize" the pope and the Vatican. If a photo-op was the goal, I didn't want our government criticized for playing such games.

It took me a while to realize what was going on. Professor Jeff Sachs of Columbia University had long positioned himself as one who would engage with Vatican policy discussions on issues such as climate, poverty, and human trafficking. I never knew whether he brought money with him, but he was often one to help define the agenda. He often prepared the concluding notes on meetings he was invited to attend and was generally helpful to a couple of Vatican offices, one being the Pontifical Academy of Sciences.

Sachs served as an advisor to the Sanders campaign and was able to convince Bishop Sanchez Sorondo that an invitation to candidate Senator Sanders would be a boost to the conference on social economy.

Senator Sanders attended the meeting and made a presentation. The symposium was on the encyclical *Centesimus Annus*, issued by Pope John Paul II on the occasion of the one-hundredth anniversary of Pope Leo XIII's encyclical *Rerum Novarum*. It seemed a stretch for a Jewish guy from Vermont, but in his presentation, he made a strong connection between his policy statements and the encyclical.

I was less concerned with what he had to say than where he showed up in the news. I had learned that he was staying at Casa Santa

Marta, the lodge inside Vatican City, where the pope also resides. (He had to sign a waiver to forgo Secret Service protection since they were not allowed inside Vatican City without approval.) It was in the plan that the pope would either attend part of the conference or appear for a photo-op. Neither happened. Following his presentation, the senator gave a brief press conference outside the Vatican gate right next to Casa Santa Marta. I stopped to greet him and his wife on my way out. I left with the feeling that all was well. I would not have to face down such questions as, *Why had I arranged for the senator to attend this Vatican meeting?* and *Why was he invited, and were any other candidates invited?*

I knew that the pope was due to leave on a short trip to the island of Lesbos, Greece, the next day to visit the refugees arriving by raft. But as things unfolded, indeed Senator Sanders happened to be in the lobby of Casa Santa Marta as the Holy Father came down to leave at about 6:00 a.m. They greeted each other, but there were no cameras, at least from the press.

My staff and I expected to hear from the Clinton and Trump campaigns. Thankfully, it never happened, because I would have been equally required to block any use of the pope as a campaign contribution to anyone's campaign.

Nevertheless, at times the PAS/PASS helped deflect from the pope those who wished to visit him, simply because they thought they deserved a private audience. One of the many from the United States in Rome who sought my help was Linda Douglass, the wife of the United States ambassador to Italy, John Philips. On one occasion, she informed me of the actor Steve Coogan, who along with Harvey Weinstein had produced the movie *Philomena*, which was showing in theatres across America and starring Judi Dench as Philomena Lee. The film was based on the true-life story of an Irish unwed mother whose child was given away to adoptive parents by the Catholic sisters who took her in. It was set in the early twentieth century and life in the Irish home was depicted as harsh and even brutal, and in no way complimentary to the Catholic Church.

Coogan, on behalf of himself and the Weinstein Group, wanted me to set up a papal audience with the real Philomena (whom he had brought with him). Coogan and Philomena wanted a private viewing of the film to be attended by the pope. The box sales were waning and this would be free advertising. I declined to commit and went to the Vatican to advise them of the request that Coogan and the Weinstein Group had made. When no action was taken by the appropriate Vatican offices, I assumed that they would make an end-run around the embassy, as our initial communications had not been amicable; there was even the suggestion by Mr. Coogan that I could lose my job, since "obviously, you don't know who you are dealing with."

The PAS/PASS served to placate Mr. Coogan, as the film was shown in the beautiful theatre inside Casino Pio IV. The chancellor attended the viewing and stated, "The pope knows the I am here with you." Later, Philomena alone greeted the pope after a Mass in what is known as *baciamano*, the kiss of the hand. It made the news in the United States, but at least it wasn't the original circus that had been planned.

This is just a small glimpse of the machinations and games to gain the limelight that a popular pope attracts. Whenever ambassadors to the Holy See gather, we often recount tales of the attempts to bully our embassies into gaining access for high profile personalities. I sympathize with the often-short-staffed curia folks who have to pull themselves away from regular duties because this or that ambassador seeks a favor.

11

THE DIPLOMATIC CORPS

ONCE I WAS APPOINTED as the United States ambassador to the Holy See, my agenda immediately became filled with ambassadors and representatives wanting to meet. The natural NATO allies presumed primacy of place followed by the "Four Eyes"—Australia, Canada, New Zealand, and the United Kingdom. The ambassador for Israel also requested early meetings. The ambassadors and representatives from Asian, Latin America, and Africa were less forthright in this regard.

Building Bridges

Ambassadors Nigel Baker from the United Kingdom, Irena Vaišvilaité from Lithuania, and Bruno Joubert from France were most helpful as I settled into the Vatican post. Nigel was formerly the ambassador to Bolivia. Before that he served as assistant private secretary to the Prince of Wales and was then appointed deputy head of mission, Havana. He was masterful at protocol and process and had taken on the Vatican position very studiously and with great professionalism.

Irena came from a career in academia and a presidential advisor in her country. As a church historian, the post as Lithuanian ambassador was ideal. She had a wealth of background on the Catholic Church in general, and specifically the Vatican. She also offered insight into the motivations and machinations of the Russians, which she really understood from having lived under Soviet rule during the Cold War. She also spent considerable time in the United States and, as such, had an appreciation of the American current political dynamic.

Bruno was born in Cambridge, Massachusetts, while his father was studying at MIT. That was the first thing we had in common. Second, he had a connection with Africa, similar to my assignments with CRS. He served in the French foreign office Africa section, as ambassador to Morocco and as Africa advisor to President Nicholas Sarkozy. A wise and skilled diplomat, we shared many things in common. He understood the strategy of "touch and go," that is, how to accomplish your agenda at a diplomatic reception tactfully while not staying late into the night. It was almost impossible to participate in every invitation extended to our embassy. Knowing how to enter at the right moment and greet the right people did allow for the possibility to attend two maybe three events in an evening. These were occasions to collect and impart the pertinent information to the right individual.

For many smaller countries, it was important for the United States to show up, and I would often honor their invitations. Ambassador Joubert had insight into certain Vatican events and matters that I treasured. He was very close to many of the French cardinals and clergy in the curia. Two were well known and highly respected: Roger Cardinal Etchegaray, the emeritus archbishop of Marseille, a former head of the Pontifical Council for Justice and Peace, and the then vice dean of the College of Cardinals, was greatly respected throughout the curia; and Jean-Louis Cardinal Tauran, who hailed from Bordeaux and headed the Pontifical Council for Inter Religious Dialogue.

During my term, particularly in the early months, these ambassadors all offered a treasure chest of geographic and diplomatic experience. I welcomed their advice and perhaps because of that they were open to giving it.

The diplomatic community was close at the Vatican. There was nothing to compete for or wrangle about. We would see each other regularly at liturgies and receptions and were generally willing to share experiences and insights.

Later, I took counsel from the Indonesian ambassador Budiarman Bahar and the Japanese ambassador, Teruki Nagasaki, who became a golfing friend. His successor, Ambassador Yoshio Matthew Nakamura, was an economic advisor to Prime Minister Shinto Abe and a visiting professor at my undergraduate university, Boston College. This was another connection that led to a solid relationship.

I found other engaging professionals throughout my tour. Ambassador Theo Loko of Benin wanted to become a deacon in the Catholic Church. I found a program for him at Pope John XXIII Seminary in Boston. He was a career diplomat, a legal scholar, and an accomplished organist. He wrote homilies for his bishop and was tuned into what was happening in parts of the Vatican and in Africa.

Armindo Fernandes do Espírito Santo Vieira, ambassador of Angola, was prudent and informed. He was former internal security head in Angola, and halfway into our tour he became the dean of the Diplomatic Corps. The dean of the Diplomatic Corps basically represents the majority and minority views of the diplomatic community to the nation to which the corps is accredited. It can be a passive or active role. Ambassador Armindo was actively engaged, and we were pleased with how he represented and dealt with information common to the entire diplomatic corps.

Similarly, Ambassador Georges El Khoury of Lebanon came from the senior leadership of his security service. During the long hiatus without a Lebanese president, his name was often mentioned as a possible contender for that position. He deftly demurred at any such speculation. However, the Vatican viewed the political situation in Lebanon of significant importance for the Middle East. Its government is a parliamentary democracy where leadership is divided by religious affiliation—the president is a Maronite Christian, the speaker of the parliament a Shi'a Muslim, and the prime minister a Sunni Muslim.

On occasion, because of my position, we were honored to meet such influential figures as Lech Walesa of Poland at the Polish Embassy. President Michel Martelly of Haiti and his wife, whom I had met in Port au Prince following the earthquake in 2010, attended a Mass at St. Peter's Basilica one Sunday.

The archbishop of Canterbury, Justin Welby, was also a regular visitor and would often worship at one of the parishes we attended on Sundays.

And in an odd and somewhat uncomfortable moment, I introduced myself to President Robert Mugabe—sanctions aside for the moment—after a Mass at St. Peter's. I then introduced John Podesta from the White House and President Mugabe refused to shake his hand. Not all diplomacy is agreeable; being politically adept, however, means that it always appears a pleasant exchange.

The Asantehene

Another memorable person was Sir James Kwame Bebaako-Mensah, Ghana's first ambassador to the Holy See, whom we would see at official functions and receptions. At one such reception, we found ourselves chatting off to the side. He knew I had spent time in Ghana and that I would appreciate the import of the Asantehene, Otumfuo Nana Osei Tutu II, visiting from his country to meet the pope. Osei Tutu II was the sixteenth traditional ruler of the Ashanti Empire. I congratulated him on the important visitor he would be receiving, but he was worried about his hosting duties: the Asantehene liked to golf, but the ambassador knew nothing about the game nor was he versed in arranging a golf date for a king who ruled eleven million inhabitants of Ghana.

Of course, he happened to be talking to the right person. I said I would be happy to take him out for a round. The ambassador was immediately and visibly relieved. We arranged the time and place and a few days later I met the Asantehene at the Cavalieri Hilton in Rome.

Out he came with his khakis and polo shirt, and we went with our respective entourages, a convoy of about ten cars. One would have thought it was Tiger Woods and Phil Mickelson!

We had reserved the tee time through Raniero Nasalli Rocca, who works at the U.S. Embassy's tri-mission finance section. He is from one of Rome's well-known families and is a member at Acqua Santa Golf Course and a fine golfer in his own right. The Acqua Santa Golf Course is on the Appian Way to the south of Rome and allows players to tee off among the ancient aqueducts that once brought the city its water.

While Raniero could not accompany us, the club pro set everything up and joined us for the round. We must have looked like something out of the "Triumphal March" from Verdi's opera *Aida*—the Asantehene and me in one cart, the club pro in another, followed by two of the Asantehene's bodyguards, trailed by my bodyguards, with the Asantehene's photographer and assistant bringing up the rear.

The Asantehene was a good golfer and very pleasant company. It was a memorable and enjoyable afternoon. That evening at a reception in the king's honor, we met him and his queen in full traditional dress, shaded by an ornate ceremonial umbrella as he entered the room.

I recalled the long, unusual journey that had taken a former volunteer with the Peace Corps in Ghana to a golf course in Rome playing a round of this Scottish game with Ghana's most important traditional leader.

Other Diplomats

We also enjoyed the company and advice of the Brazilian ambassador, Denis Fontes De Souza Pinto and his wife, Maria. Denis was wonderfully adept at gaining access into certain quarters in the curia manned by Brazilians, of which there were many.

If you really wanted to know what was going on, one had to consult Ambassador Georgios Poulides. George had his finger on many pulses as the ambassador from Cyprus. Though his small apartment residence was cramped, everyone wanted to be invited, as his dinners were wonderfully revealing. He has now become the dean of the Diplomatic Corps at the Vatican.

The Russian ambassador, Aleksandr Avdeyev, was more problematic. My meetings with him were often awkward and restrained. After the Russian invasion of Ukraine and the takeover of the Crimea, we found no common ground or agreement. However, what I found most interesting was that he traveled frequently around Italy as a promoter or representative of the Russian Orthodox Church to local Catholic bishops.

Some of the residences of the Vatican ambassadors are massive and historically prominent, while others are unobtrusive in their simplicity. We found ourselves most at home around the crowded dining room tables of Ambassador Tamara Grdzelidze of Georgia, or that of Ambassador Tetiana Izhevska of Ukraine, or in a small restaurant just a few blocks from Ambassador Irena Vaišvilaitė's apartment.

The English-speaking group of ambassadors naturally gravitated toward one another. Ambassador Dennis Savoie, the Canadian ambassador, was both a neighbor and a friend. He was the number two at the Knights of Columbus in New Haven, Connecticut, for several years. He and his wife, Claudette, quickly developed Canadian connections in the Vatican and in town. Prior to his arrival, his embassy was closed by the former prime minister for economic reasons and perhaps some unspoken controversy with the Vatican. Dennis reopened the embassy and his new, young prime minister, Justin Trudeau, seemed to approve. Interestingly, there was another representative from Canada. Quebec maintains a person who claims to be in Rome to sponsor their interests. I was never certain whether the Holy See recognized the individual.

Ambassador John McCarthy from Australia was literally larger than life. With his Australian cowboy hat and his six-foot, four-inch frame, he was physically imposing. Having had limited contact with Australians, I didn't realize how much they value their relations with us, and how often they fought with us in wars around the world.

As we noted in the previous chapter, John was very active in the Vatican's efforts to end human trafficking. With a wife who was a concert pianist, he hosted entertaining concerts at his residence. John was also a cricket enthusiast and organized the Vatican cricket team. He was proud to accompany them on tour and join in on their team anthem "Ave Maria," sung in Latin. We ourselves had a chance to cheer on the pontifical football team in the Clericus Cup, an annual soccer tournament among the priests and seminarians of Rome's pontifical universities. The Americans, being numerous, had a very good team. They almost always advanced to the semifinals, and they had the best cheering squad. On one occasion, however, when the American seminarians played the French, even though we won, the French were handing out cheese and sausage to the fans. On that day, they won first prize for spirit in the stands.

The Latin American ambassadors formed a tight-knit group and, since I could not speak Spanish, we never became close, apart from Ambassador Carlos Avila Molina. He was the former minister of education in Honduras and a former baseball player for the national team.

At all official ceremonies and liturgies at the Vatican, ambassadors are seated in the order in which they presented their credentials to the pope. Ambassador Molina presented his credentials just eight days before me. He also had a daughter working in Seattle and a son who is a doctor in Texas. So, we always had a topic of conversation.

Women Ambassadors

The number of women ambassadors grew significantly during my term. Of the eighty-six resident embassies and missions to the Holy See, thirteen were headed by extremely competent and accomplished women. Ambassador Tamara Grdzelidze of Georgia, for example, is an Orthodox theologian who had spent many years at the World Council of Churches. I turned to her often for counsel and explanations on various Orthodox matters.

Given our special interest in supporting the Ukrainian government following the Maidan Revolution in 2014, I spent considerable time with Ukrainian Ambassador Tetiana Izhevska. She would brief us on changes taking place in the country. When I was able to invite Geoffrey Pyatt, the then United States ambassador to Ukraine, on two occasions to brief the Secretariat of State regarding the U.S.

position on events in Ukraine, I made sure that Ambassador Tetiana was welcomed to many of the dinners and events that I held. When the Russians invaded Crimea in 2014, many former Soviet countries came together. The ambassadors for Poland, Ukraine, Lithuania, and Georgia, all approached me in solidarity, hoping that the United States would respond with more than sanctions. I listened and empathized with them and conveyed their views to Washington.

Ambassador Mónica Jiménez de la Jara from Chile was not a trained diplomat but had served as the minister of education and the president of the Catholic University of Temuco as well as other positions. Together, with others, we sponsored various panels on the role of women in the Church and women in conflict situations. Another ambassador, Emma Madigan of Ireland, a career diplomat, was also eager to sponsor and participate in such events. She was given the somewhat unenviable task of reopening the Irish Embassy by herself. The embassy was closed in 2011 ostensibly for financial reasons, but at the same time, relations between Church and state in Ireland had deteriorated markedly after the cover-up of sexual abuse in the Church.

Emma, with her husband, also a diplomat (on leave), and preschool son, were alone in finding a chancery building, purchasing all the needed furniture, all without much support from the home office. In fact, the former Irish Embassy to the Holy See, Villa Spada, had been located on the Gianicolo Hill three buildings away from my residence. Said to be one of Ireland's most luxurious, the Irish Embassy to Italy took that building as its chancery and residence.

One of our most entertaining colleagues, Ambassador Miroslava Rosa Vargas from Panama, told us that she had one primary objective when she arrived, to get the pope to visit Panama. Nothing would block her path, which she paved with smart, witty maneuverings, and she succeeded. Additionally, she was the life of every gathering. Many diplomats don't exhibit much zeal but rather a measured restraint. Miroslava was the opposite. Clearly, her demeanor was genuine and very effective, as the pope visited Panama in early 2019.

The Mechanics of Diplomacy

Each geographic region—Europe, Asia, Africa, and Latin America—had their own groups where they met regularly, surfaced common concerns, and elected an ambassador to represent their views to the Secretariat of State. The Canada and the United States were left out of the mix. When I asked Cardinal Parolin how he wanted to deal with us, I suggested that the Secretariat hold periodic briefings with us and the diplomatic corps. He pushed back and asked that we simply bring our concerns directly to him and his staff. Indeed, over my term I found him and his staff most accommodating, often meeting daily to discuss issues.

Vatican diplomacy always took a path of personal relationship searching for common ground. It was never transactional as none of us had any commodity to sell or trade except sharing information, which required trust. The Holy See was not particularly forthright in offering information until a certain understanding of discretion was established. Using information for the good was part of the equation but using it to cast aspersions or to self-aggrandize always limited it.

A rapport was certainly developed with Archbishop Paul Gallagher. As I mentioned earlier, we had met in the Philippines when he served at the nunciature, situated in the noisiest place in Manila, right beneath the light-rail track on Taft Ave. He was later moved to Bujumbura, Burundi, to take over after the assassination of the apostolic nuncio, Archbishop Michael Courtney, in 2003.

As secretary for relations with states, he appreciated in me a person who had experience with many of the same situations and places where his experience lay.

By 2014, my credibility had developed and, with the help of the staff at the embassy, our integrity, so much so that information began to flow more freely. We had moved beyond the Wikileaks scandal.

In fact, at the instigation of the British ambassador, a small group of ambassadors would meet bimonthly with Archbishop Gallagher in an off-the-record (Chatham House Rule) dinner. These were exceptionally revealing because the archbishop was often coming directly from a meeting with the Holy Father.

Are There Tennis Courts at the Vatican?

When I meet someone playing tennis these days, and my days as ambassador come up, the invariable question is, "Are there tennis courts at the Vatican?" The general impression of many is that Vatican City is only chapels and columns and the works of Michelangelo, not Federer, Djokovic, or Williams. In fact, this small city makes room for recreation. Though the courts once played on in past years are now unusable, it is not because they have been given over to a religious function. They have become a storage area filled with containers and shipping pods. Still there are tennis opportunities on various church properties around Vatican City.

As I have noted, working as an ambassador to the Holy See is about relationships. And, just as with business in the United States, many relationships are formed and nourished on the tennis courts or the golf course.

By far the best among the few Vatican tennis players that I encountered was René Bruelhart, who served as the president of the board of directors of the Financial Information Authority of Vatican City (AIF). He was also something of a sandbagger. The first time we played, he admitted to being rusty, having not played in a while, but added, "I did put myself through college coaching tennis." He was good. And he held an important position in Pope Francis's effort to clean up the Vatican's finances.

I also formed a regular monthly group with seminarians from the Pontifical North American College, including Nicolaus Thai from the Diocese of Orange, California; Austin Ammanniti and David Kidd, both from the Diocese of Toledo; and Robert Boxie from the Archdiocese of Washington. Robert, a Harvard Law graduate, was above our level in intelligence and tennis talent, but he tolerated us. All were studying for advanced degrees at one of the many Pontifical Universities. And a ringer who joined us later was Fr. Justin Blanc from the Diocese of Wheeling-Charleston, West Virginia. I enjoyed playing with them, and it was a good chance to learn what was happening in and around Rome and the world of Roman academia. Most likely they also enjoyed playing with the American ambassador surrounded by his bodyguards. I owe a great deal to the rector of the North American Pontifical College. He allowed me to come anytime to use the courts or walk around the track with Joan. My bodyguards did not see the need to accompany me inside the seminary compound, and the sense of being alone, yet outdoors was a welcome "destressor."

An infrequent participant to my tennis group was Kishore Jayabalam, the director of the Istituto Acton, the Acton Institute's office in Rome.[1] The Acton Institute represents more conservative views than my own, but we managed to steer clear of politics in our "between-sets" chats. Kishore, having once served in the Pontifical Council for Justice and Peace, had good insights and connections in and about the Vatican.

In addition, Ambassador Tomaz Kunstelj of Slovenia was an entertaining and good player who filled us in on scuttlebutt when candidate Donald Trump entered the scene. Trump's wife, Melania, was from Slovenia. In such a small country, everybody knew each other. Tomaz also seemed to have connections in the curia that were unknown to many of us, and he often shared his insights on the court.

Toward the end of my term, we were joined by Dr. Alessandro Olivi, the director of neurosurgery at Policlinico Gemelli. Alex, who spent several years at Johns Hopkins School of Medicine, was introduced to me in Baltimore by my physician, Mark Saba, himself a tennis player. The courts became a microcosm of the city-state and served to open the flow of information and local color.

The Art of Golf

Anyone who has played golf knows that four hours on the links is a great way to get to know someone. For me, that included some members of the curia as well as diplomats and others.

I learned a great deal about some of the courses around Rome from Greg Burke, who was appointed vice director of the Holy See Press Office in December 2015, and then promoted to director on August 1, 2016. He introduced me to the Acqua Santa, Parco di Roma, Marco Simone (the site of the 2022 Ryder Cup), and Castel Gandolfo Golf Club courses. When he was senior communications advisor to the Secretariat of State, he had some weekends off. Once he took up his new position, it was tough to get a place on his schedule, but we still managed to hit the little white ball around a few times.

Playing with the mouthpiece of the Vatican had its advantages, but Greg was discrete and did not let too much slip unless it was an answer—or nonanswer to a direct question.

In 2016, the word was out that Fr. Seamus Horgan, an Irish priest working in the second section of the Secretariat of State, was an avid golfer. He had recently arrived from an assignment at the nunciature in the Philippines. This gave us a natural connection because I had also spent five years based in Manila working for CRS. He lived inside Vatican City at Casa Santa Marta. He was a great source of fun and information, and important news or events were explained in greater depth thanks to his knowledge, his proximity to the center, and to his Irish wit.

Seamus was a great raconteur and jokester. He told us how he kept his clubs in his room and was very careful to be especially surreptitious in sneaking them down the elevator to his car when he went to play. He thought he had succeeded in keeping his pastime a secret. After he had been at the Vatican about six months, the pope met him one day on his way to the office and asked, "How's the golf game?"

Seamus was "the desk officer" for the Indian subcontinent, Oceania, and the Philippines, an area that comprises over 350 dioceses. With a workday plate as full as this, a good game of golf with a cigar was for him just what his doctor ordered to alleviate the stress.

We were able to play an occasional game with Msgr. Bob Oliver, the secretary of the Pontifical Commission for the Protection of Minors, who was from the Archdiocese of Boston. He spent much of his time traveling the globe in his position to work with bishops' conferences explaining best standards and practices.

The American Parish

There are about eight churches in Rome where one can attend an English-speaking Mass. The most well-known to Americans was

Santa Susanna just a few blocks from the American Embassy to Italy (and eventually, in September 2015, Embassy Vatican).

The "American parish," as Santa Susanna was known, had its beginnings in the 1920s. The superior general of the Paulist Fathers traveled to the Vatican, meeting with Pope Benedict XV to gain formal papal recognition for the Paulist Fathers. At the time, they were recognized only as a religious community in the United States by the American bishops. While their superior general was in Rome, he was on the lookout for a church that could be considered an American parish and one that the Paulist Fathers would staff. He found one—Santa Susanna Church—close to the United States Embassy to Italy located on Via Veneto.

Apparently, he acquired the blessing of Pope Benedict XV and, upon his return, found a way to make his request to President Harding. The president, although not a Catholic, took up the idea and the apostolic nuncio in Washington asking that there be an American parish in Rome and specifically mentioned Santa Susanna.

For many decades thereafter, through the Second World War, there was an American parish at Santa Susanna Church staffed by the Paulist Fathers. While the property of the church and land on which it sat remained with the Cistercian Order, the Paulist Fathers were given full right of use by the vicariate in Rome. Furthermore, the cardinal archbishops of Boston accepted it as their titular church.

The concept of *titular*, or title, to churches arose from the fifth-century tradition of giving older churches to patron families, who maintained them. Later, these churches became assigned to cardinals who were, in the past, chosen from the clergy of Rome. These days, cardinals are appointed from around the world. To symbolize their ties with Rome, all cardinals are honored with a titular church in the city of Rome. Given that local parishes and religious congregations own these church properties, the vicariate assigns church usage while also bestowing foreign cardinals with titles to them; confusion about who is in charge abounds.

Fast forward to 2012. A small group of aged Cistercian nuns, living in the convent attached to Santa Susanna Church, protested the presence of the American parish next door. The nuns wanted the

Paulist Fathers, and their parish, out. There were various nonsensical reasons for this need to vacate—I never got a satisfactory answer as to why these Cistercian nuns felt such animus as to demand that the parish vacate the church.

By the time we arrived in Rome, the parish had temporally moved and was accommodated in the parish of Camillus de Lellis, just a block from the embassy. Apparently, the Cistercian nuns had received a fire inspection report that deemed the Santa Susanna Church unsafe. Meanwhile, the Paulist Fathers and resident parish community were in the process of lodging a spirited attempt to reverse the position of the nuns—never an easy undertaking.

As the American ambassador and a parish attendee, I was enlisted to support the cause. Rightly, the parish was started based on the request of the American President Warren Harding to the Holy See, and it was partially my role to defend the parish's existence and good functioning. I engaged the secretary of state on the matter, and it wound its way through the Vatican offices and to the vicariate of Rome, which is the body that handles such matters.

The eventual solution was relocation to an Irish parish, St. Patrick's, one street north of the embassy. After long negotiations, in 2016, St. Patrick's became the new home of the American parish in Rome.

Outdoor Liturgies

Of course, as diplomats, we were expected to attend formal Masses at St. Peter's Basilica, primarily when the Holy Father was celebrating the liturgy. Inside the basilica, diplomats are seated together in a special section to the left of the altar as you faced it; outside, on the steps in front of St. Peter's, we are seated to the right of the altar with heads of state and other civil dignitaries. We witnessed canonizations, the Jubilee Year of Mercy, the opening of the Holy Door, and the magnificent Palm Sunday processions, among so many other holy celebrations, all of which are part of ancient ritual and choreographed to inspire prayer.

There were two occasions when we were seated outside that I suffered a good sunburn on my face and head. While we were dressed in formal wear, none of the male ambassadors wore a hat. If you put up an umbrella against the sun, you blocked the view of those behind.

I had had enough with sunburns. A small group of balding ambassadors decided that while it may not be the absolute proper protocol, a hat was called for. But who would go first? I decided to take the plunge, wearing a somber short-brimmed cap. If the American ambassador could do it, why not us? Consequently, there followed a half dozen or so ambassadors wearing caps during the sunny outdoor liturgies.

A Church for the Poor

Early in his tenure Pope Francis called upon the Church and particularly the clergy to "move to the peripheries." He counseled priests, saying, "I want to see sand on your shoes not a shine." He wanted a poor Church for the poor where we invited the poorest among us and not dictate mandates of how they should live.

I offer a few examples of those who Pope Francis encouraged to reach out to the peripheries and whom I had the privilege of meeting.

Charity and Dignity

A wealthy couple who are friends of mine visited Rome in early 2014 and said they would really like to donate to one of the Holy Father's important charities and asked my advice. I made an appointment with Archbishop Krajewski.

We walked to the almoner's office and told the nun at the counter that we had an appointment with the archbishop and asked if he was in. She said he was coming immediately but we could wait in his office. We had the opportunity to peek in at the office that pressed the stamps for the papal blessings on the parchment that were sent to people across the globe who requested them, usually for marriages, anniversaries, or birthdays. It was a small room no more than ten square feet.

In his waiting room were a couple of espresso makers in boxes, and other nonsubstantive gifts piled along the wall. There was a bit of disorder about the place, but I dismissed it as a lack of space.

When Archbishop Krajewski arrived, he was apologetic and immediately sat down with Mario Mesquita, my deputy chief of mission, and myself. We asked how his operation worked trying to gather a sense of how best to apply the one-million-dollar donation from this wealthy couple. I never let on that the million was in the back of my mind.

The archbishop got up from his chair and grabbed some envelopes, showing the pope's miniature scribble, "take care of this," on gifts of five to ten thousand dollars in all currencies. Coming from the American nonprofit bureaucracy, I asked him about the accountability to the donor. He answered in a perplexed way that we do what the pope asks. My immediate reaction was that this is not going to fly with American donors. They want to know specifically how their gift is to be applied.

Essentially, adopting a Mother Teresa approach, he stated, "We are not here to adjust the structural problems that need to be addressed; we are here to respond with immediate charity and care. Others are more qualified to address the causal issues of homelessness. But the Holy Father doesn't hesitate to speak about it on a regular basis."

The archbishop was noted for his concern for the homeless. He installed showers, improved the toilets around the outside of the Vatican walls, he arranged for a barber, distributed sleeping bags, and invited the homeless to a yearly concert at the Sistine Chapel. It was all about respect for the individuals and their individual dignity.

A Church on the Peripheries

Fr. Bill Headley was a professor at Duquesne University when I invited him to work with us on peacebuilding at CRS. In fact, I asked him to initiate and lead a new strategic direction for us in this area.

Bill had significant experience in Africa and introduced us to his own community, the Spiritans, who are based in Africa, Asia, Europe, and the United States. They have a special charism of taking on a missionary challenge and quickly handing it over to the local church. Sometimes that works great and quickly, other times it takes more time. They also own Duquesne University in Pittsburgh.

After nearly five years with us at CRS, Bill was asked to become founding dean of the Kroc School of Peace Studies at the University of San Diego. Leaving CRS left us with a hole, but I was proud of the contributions he made at focusing us on peacebuilding.

The Central African Republic is a tortured place. In the 1970s, Jean-Bédel Bokassa led a coup that literally turned the country into his empire. Following his ouster, life for the everyday folks didn't improve much, but as things deteriorated on its border with Sudan and weak governments grabbed all the resources they could, internal strife with a faux religious label plagued the country. Massacres became normal in the capital Bangui and around the country. Muslims fled into Chad and Cameroon, and Christians and animists to wherever they could find succor. The government was almost helpless and certainly useless. The French military arrived, but the situation had become too chaotic for their presence to solve the problem.

Emerging from decades of this chaos was the brave Catholic archbishop Dieudonné (Gift of God) Nzapalainga. At forty-eight years old, he was young to be an archbishop in the Catholic Church. He was a Spiritan, the same religious order as Fr. Bill Headley. There had been some major problems in the previous decade among the bishops. Thus, in 2009, he was appointed as apostolic administrator of Bangui diocese, and then, in 2012, made archbishop.

Some Christians, or more appropriately "some thugs," perpetrated a wave of violence against Muslims. Amid the war, Archbishop Dieudonné invited the religious leaders—including the Muslims and Protestant evangelicals—to act together to address the growing unrest in the country. In fact, he invited the imam to stay with him in his residence. Since then, they have continued to persuade Muslims, Catholics, and Protestants to avoid further violence. They have been working together tirelessly to restore the social fabric of their country by addressing the root causes of mistrust in remote villages.

In November 2015, against the warnings of many, Pope Francis visited Bangui. His visit had a specific calming impact on the tensions in the country. A year later, he named Archbishop Nzapalainga a cardinal, representing his desire for a church to go to the peripheries.

Caritas Internationalis

The headquarters of Caritas Internationalis resides in one of the Vatican properties outside the walls of Vatican City. Their network is supported by a small staff in Rome who offer a convening role to the membership and others. They generally do not provide any direct service but rather support its individual members, for example, Caritas Italy or Caritas programs in other programs that assist their local communities.

The then director general, Dr. Michel Roy, is a French national, and the staff includes several Americans, whom I knew from my days at CRS. They brought the organization into contact with the embassy.

The strength of Caritas is that it builds from the community or parish to the diocesan/district level and then to a national level. They generally stay very close to the local people and have special access and insight on events. Furthermore, when a situation gets bad, Caritas groups, often with other Catholic or faith-based groups that are "on the ground," usually mount an early response. Such was the case with two events that occurred during my tenure in Rome.

In late 2013, cases of the Ebola virus were identified in the West African nation of Guinea.[2] Given the paucity and lack of sophistication of medical care, the disease spread rapidly. It did not respect borders and soon reached into Sierra Leone, Liberia, and other locations in West Africa, Europe, and even the United States.

The Catholic medical facilities with the help of Caritas and its foreign partners rapidly mounted a response as best they could. In Sierra Leone, the principle Catholic response was from the St. John of God Hospital in Lunsar, close to the border with Guinea.[3] In Liberia, the locus of the Caritas response was at Catholic Hospital of Saint Joseph in Monrovia.[4] Wherever possible, there were coordinated response efforts with local governments and medical facilities run by other faith groups. Over two years, there were 28,600 cases identified with 11,325 deaths.

CI held a very important and useful meeting in 2015 at its headquarters in Piazza San Calisto in Rome. They convened ambassadors, medical professionals, and some journalists to listen to a briefing by Caritas and other Catholic representatives from Guinea, Liberia, and Sierra Leone. Most memorable was the presentation of Sr. Barbara Brillant, a Franciscan sister, who headed Liberia's National Catholic Health Care Council.[5] She was clear and powerful about what needed to be done. Having lived in Liberia for thirty-six years, she knew well the frustrations as well as the generosity and resilience of the Liberian people. She spelled out some of the problems extending beyond the epidemic, such as convincing families to isolate the sick, dispelling the stigma associated with the afflicted, and separation of families from burial. Just discerning a normal intestinal illness from Ebola and treating it was becoming problematic. Her basic premise, since no vaccine was available, was the need for training and retraining to keep the staff safe and curtail the spread of the disease. Dispelling certain cultural traditions and treating the whole person became a workable solution. Being able to hear Sr. Barbara on Skype and get the reality from the sources on the ground was a great service that allowed us to report to our respective countries.

The U.S. military had just made a commitment to assist in Liberia. But in her briefing, Sr. Barbara, while praising their good intentions, did not hesitate to critique their response as often misdirected and uninformed. Present at the briefing was Dr. Tim Flanigan, an infectious disease specialist from Providence, Rhode Island. He is affiliated with multiple hospitals in the area, including Miriam Hospital and Rhode Island Hospital as well as Alpert Medical School at Brown University. He was just finishing a two-month volunteer stint in Liberia to help with the disease response. I'm sure he carried that message back to the military and CDC to help guide the U.S. military's efforts more sensibly.

For many years, Msgr. Bob Vitillo worked in various capacities with Caritas Internationalis in Rome as well as with the U.S. Bishop's Campaign for Human Development and the Permanent Observer Mission of the Holy See to the United Nations Office and Specialized Agencies in Geneva. Bob was instrumental in the late '80 and early '90s in calling attention to the scourge of HIV/AIDS. He spent considerable energy in traveling to various bishops' conferences and Caritas organizations explaining the impact of the disease. That was at a moment before there was much openness toward accepting the fact that the disease was not only affecting homosexuals, which was the knee-jerk response during that period. Of course, he was prophetic.

Bob remained committed to this agenda but added the Ebola crisis to it on behalf of CI. He organized many meetings on both topics and was determined to make those in the Church and beyond understand the human impacts of both these scourges.

In April 2016, Joan and I attended a meeting organized by Bob for many Caritas members on the topic of Pediatric AIDS.[6] Only in the few years prior to this meeting was the topic gaining the attention it needed and Caritas, and the Catholic Church were some of the strongest voices engaged on the topic. On the podium was Dr. Mark Dybul, the executive director of the Global Fund for HIV/AIDS, Dr. Deborah Birx, the U.S. global coordinator, and Dr. Luiz Loures, who was the deputy executive director of the Joint United Nations Programme on HIV/AIDS. One after the other, they heaped praise citing specific examples that the work of Caritas and the Catholic Church had accomplished through its integral approach to the entire person while addressing the clinical aspects of the HIV/AIDS crisis.

Msgr. Bob Vitillo, my wife, Joan, and I were proud that we had undertaken an uphill battle at CRS when we first entered the HIV/AIDS response arena in 2003. At the time, CRS had no experience in clinical medicine. Nevertheless, we partnered with the University of Maryland Institute of Human Virology to work with dozens of Catholic hospitals in Africa, adopting their integrated health-care approach. The traditional contractors for the U.S. government medical contracts, who dealt strictly with the dispensing of antiretroviral or other clinical solutions, saw us as poaching, as did USAID and, at times, the folks at CDC. To now have the three large HIV/AIDS funders talking about the powerful empirical results accomplished by a Catholic approach to people suffering with AIDS that was not just clinical but wholistic was uplifting.

12

CONGEDO

EARLY IN THE SUMMER of 2016, Joan and I began actively considering our postelection plans. I was of the view that we—or at least I—should remain until the new ambassador was announced, which most probably would be the following summer. Joan preferred to leave in January 2017. For continuity's sake, it is normal practice, irrespective of party, to remain in place if possible until the nomination. Vetting ambassadors and confirming them takes considerable time. Meanwhile continuing to maintain contacts and avoiding long vacancies in posts helps the new appointee once he or she arrives.

Our planning was put on hold, for there were other things on which to focus our attention. In September, our daughter, Jenny, was to have her wedding in Rome. Jen came to visit in late May. She and Joan began the process of finding the venues, hotel, and a caterer. I participated as much as my schedule would allow, without inserting myself into the decision-making or planning. Especially useful for my security detail was knowing which locations might be considered for the marriage and reception.

That summer was busy. The pope visited Armenia and Poland, both highly symbolic events. The matter of the Armenian genocide had been swirling around Francis from the early days of his papacy. When he first used the term *genocide* to refer to the tragedy of 1915 in Armenia, Turkey recalled its ambassador to the Holy See. Many cautioned the pope not to repeat the terminology during his Armenian visit. He claimed that he had always referred to the massacre with that term, and it would not be his desire to use another word to describe the horrible events.[1] He was reasonably close to the Armenian community living in Argentina and, as such, was well informed on the matter.

In Poland, he brought almost three million young people together for a World Youth Day Mass and celebration. He followed this event with an important visit to the Auschwitz-Birkenau concentration camp.[2]

He also visited Georgia and Azerbaijan, which was another overture to the Orthodox and to Islam as well as an attempt to cool the tensions between Azerbaijan and Armenia.

Part of our job was to examine such visits and to glean insights into what the pope might do or say that would be helpful to Washington and to our diplomats in those countries. Pope Francis traveled to many countries during his first years. He was characterized as "a pope in a hurry." From his first visit to Brazil to these last two trips before my departure, our embassy staff had a heavy workload.

Additionally, we had an extensive visitors' list ourselves, perhaps because the end of the Obama administration was in sight in this last summer of the president's term.

Toward the end of May, we hosted Shaun Casey, the special representative for religion and global affairs at the U.S. State Department, and his staff. Shortly thereafter, we hosted General Joseph Dunford, who at the time was the chairman of the joint chiefs of staff. Then, in September, we hosted a series of congressional delegations, "codels,"[3] beginning with the House Speaker Nancy Pelosi; followed by Congressman Hal Rodger's group; then a congressional group including Representatives Fortenberry, Harris, and Lipinski, all of whom were in town to attend the annual International Catholic Legislators Conference; and finally a delegation headed by Representative Kevin McCarthy.

On Labor Day weekend, my daughter's wedding guests began to arrive and prepare for the wedding for September 8. I will not expand on the wedding other than to say it was a most memorable event.

Before we realized, the election was upon us. Somewhere around the week before the election, we received an instruction from the State Department's European Bureau asking that we make clear how long we were prepared to stay on, if asked, during the upcoming administration. The information was due in Washington by December 11.

Joan and I were prepared to remain until March 2017, with an absolute end date of the first of June. By January 5, we learned that the transition team of the incoming administration had issued an advisory that all President Obama's political appointees should resign no later than January 20, 2017.[4] This worked for us, but I knew other ambassadors who had children in school or spouses working under contracts. Such a strident instruction would cause hardship. Additionally, it would vacate many ambassadorial posts, which is not a good situation.

Now, some years distant from our departure in what seemed, in my estimation, to be a chaotic and ineffective foreign policy during the Trump administration, we do not regret our decision in the least. From what I read and heard, the Department of State under the Trump administration suffered from poor morale, with many staff leaving if they could.

From what I can glean without being privy to specifics, during the Trump administration, the only areas where there was a convergence of interests between the U.S. government and those of the Holy See appeared to be religious freedom and human trafficking. On climate change, Cuba, Israel-Palestine, Syria, migration, nuclear deterrence, and a range of other issues there appears to be divergence.

Joan and I organized and began to pack. In late August, a terrible earthquake struck Amatrice, a town in the province of Rieti, in northern Lazio (central Italy). As the winter months approached, a call went out to help the mountain town's inhabitants. Our parish took up a collection for warm clothes and, as we were leaving and heading for Florida, we emptied our closets of our winter ski wear and sweaters for those living in the cold.

By November, we announced our departure and began to say our goodbyes. Beatrice Mirelli, our most competent protocol officer, informed me that we should schedule a *congedo* with the Holy Father.

I had no idea what a *congedo* was, but tradition indicated that a formal goodbye was called for. So, on January 16, 2017, we were given an appointment time, and Joan and I headed to the Apostolic Palace for the farewell. The pope greeted us and offered a small gift. With a few kind words and his questions about what was next for us, we thanked him and thus ended our wonderful time at the Vatican. He had the same demeanor of calmness, congeniality, and compassion of a pastor.

Fenway, Our Dog

One last tale involves our dog. As we booked flights out of Rome on January 20, the travel agent at the embassy was insistent that we could not bring the dog on the plane if it exceeded twenty-two pounds. We had to ensure that he was under the limit. The dog was borderline (his weight varied by the week), but I kept telling my secretary that it should not be a problem. The travel agent continued to be insistent.

On the day of departure, we said our goodbyes to the staff and headed for Rome's Leonardo da Vinci International Airport. We carried the dog to the check-in desk in the pet travel bag and registered for business class. (The State Department gives this one perk upon departure; all other trips are economy class.) Of course, my full squad of bodyguards wanted to say goodbye. That meant that there was a posse of fully armed gentlemen and one lady with us, standing with Joan, Fenway, and myself at the counter. I told the attendant that we wanted to carry the dog on with us. She looked at me, then at the bodyguards and never bothered to weigh Fenway. We said *arrivederci* to these wonderful people who had protected us for almost four years. They had become like family. And then, we departed.

Conclusions

It was a bittersweet departure. We were proud to represent our president and our country. We appreciated the engagement with other motivated individuals even when we disagreed. We enjoyed the comradery of colleagues who were smart, dedicated, and committed. I valued the opportunity to engage on important global issues, but, at the same time, we both looked forward to returning to be with our family.

I knew that the incoming president should have his own ambassador nominated and confirmed without dispatch. Happily, President Trump instructed us to leave promptly on or before January 20, and he appointed my successor relatively quickly.

The relations between the United States and the Holy See will endure and thrive. The Holy See, in fact, sees relationships not in four-year terms but as generational.

My time as ambassador during the first years of Pope Francis's pontificate was a special time in the life of the Church, the Holy See, and its relations with the United States.

The Holy See is a global power as Francis Rooney, one of my predecessors so aptly elaborates.[5] During my tenure, the "soft power" of the Holy See was visible in Cuba, to some extent, and unsuccessfully in Venezuela. In the Central African Republic, there were initial steps toward a peace after the papal visit. In Ukraine, Iraq, the Holy Land, and at the climate meeting in Paris, Vatican soft power was very apparent. The representatives of the Holy See find it best to work quietly rather than on the public stage. That experience has taught them that the limelight is fleeting. These days, the Holy See has stepped into complex negotiations with China, but they have been involved with this for decades. As a Vatican official told me, "We are not in a rush."

My observation is that they know what they are doing and, in each instance, have a plan. It may move slowly, but it is not tied to a budget year or a specific, finite tour of duty.

Their manner of action was often hard to appreciate because many of us had a limited term and wanted things accomplished on our watch. In my case, the FATCA agreement, the Cuba deal, some progress regarding human trafficking, and the relocation of the embassy worked out. Other matters, such as Ukraine, Middle East peace, and the problems in Venezuela are yet to be resolved.

Admittedly, my four years with Pope Francis were the halcyon years. Negative criticism toward him began in 2014 and continued after the publication of *Laudato Si'*. It increased further after the publication of *Amoris Laetitia*—a time when there were those who felt he had gone too far from traditional doctrine on marriage and divorce.[6] This rejection does not represent anywhere near the views of a majority of laity and clerics who approve his teaching of mercy.

The concept of mercy, which was the motivation for him calling for a Holy Year of Mercy,[7] is vital and integral to everything he does. Some are uncomfortable with this approach, but this will be his legacy and the guiding principle in his choices for new cardinals and bishops. He speaks about going to the peripheries, where one can find pastors who are merciful: *miserando atque eligendo* (out of mercy you are chosen).[8]

The future leadership of the Holy See will most likely follow the trail that Francis has blazed. It represents a path oriented toward the realities that people face rather than doctrine alone. The Catholic Church in Africa is growing faster than anywhere else in the world and will make its imprint. In many ways, it will be considered by the North Americans and Europeans as more theologically conservative, even though it is culturally more tolerant.

The Vatican watches administrations in countries come and go. It will explore convergent opportunities with our future administrations, and if alignment on policy is not found, it will hold to its own path at its own pace. Its vision is the long term, or the "eschatological," not the budget year.

At the time of writing, there were 122 cardinal "electors"—that is, those below the age of eighty who may vote for the next pope. Of that group, 58 percent have been appointed by Pope Francis. A two-thirds majority is necessary to elect a new pope. One might expect that some appointed by Pope Benedict XVI or even St. John Paul II might wish to follow Pope Francis's legacy and others appointed by Francis might not. Nevertheless, his legacy is secure and will be lasting.

Hopefully Pope Francis's successor will continue to be a beacon of tolerance, understanding, and mercy—a pope who holds firm to the truth but listens compassionately to all views while exhibiting a special sensitivity to the poor and marginalized people.

The period during the second term of President Obama and the first four years of the pontificate of Pope Francis was unique. There were so many areas where policy positions converged. Generally, the Obama administration, while not totally aligned with the Holy See on everything, were close on most areas of policy.

The posture of the Obama administration toward the Holy See closely matched that of President Reagan; in both cases, much was achieved for the global good. Hopefully, future presidents will recognize the special global position that the Holy See and a pope like Francis presents.

NOTES

Introduction

1. Catholic News Service, "Shuttle Diplomacy: Kerry and Vatican's Parolin: In Whirlwind Conference, They Discuss Syria, Mideast, U.S. Health Mandate," *America*, January 14, 2014, https://www.americamagazine.org/issue/shuttle-diplomacy-kerry-and-vaticans-parolin.

2. Ben Rhodes, *The World as It Is* (New York: Random House, 2018), 284–89, 300–304.

3. Eileen Egan, *Catholic Relief Services: The Beginning Years* (Baltimore: Catholic Relief Services, 1988); Catholic Relief Services, *For Whom There Is No Room* (Mahwah, NJ: Paulist Press, 1995).

4. Associated Press, "Pope Francis Hints He May Not Be around in 2019," *Crux*, April 8, 2017, https://cruxnow.com/vatican/2017/04/pope-francis-hints-may-not-around-2019.

5. Giancarlo Elia Valori, "The Vatican and the Russian Federation," *Modern Diplomacy*, September 6, 2019; Victor Gaetan, "Pope Francis Holy Diplomacy in Ukraine," *Foreign Affairs*, September 5, 2019.

6. Elisabetta Piqué, *Pope Francis: Life and Revolution* (Chicago: Loyola Press 2013); Nello Scavo, *Bergolio's List* (Gastonia, NC: Saint Benedict's Press, 2014); Luis Rosales and Daniel Olivera, *Francis: A Pope for Our Time* (Boca Raton, FL: Humanix

Books, 2013); Austen Ivereigh, *The Great Reformer* (London: Allen & Unwin, 2014); Paul Valley, *Pope Francis: The Struggle for the Soul of Catholicism* (New York: Bloomsbury, 2015); Marco Politi, *Pope Francis among the Wolves* (New York: Columbia University Press, 2015); David Willey, *The Promise of Francis* (New York: Gallery Books, 2015); Jimmy Burns, Francis, *Pope of Good Promise* (New York: St. Martin's Press, 2015).

1. The White Smoke

1. See the College of Cardinals, Vatican website, http://www .vatican.va/roman_curia/cardinals/index.htm.

2. Gianluigi Nuzzi, *Sua Santità. Le carte segrete di Benedetto XVI* (Milan: Chiarelettere, 2012).

2. The Vatican—a Global Entity

1. Nicolas Seneze, *Comment l'Amerique veut changer de pape* (Paris: Bayard, 2019).

2. See Jimmy Burns, *Francis, Pope of Good Promise* (New York: St. Martin's Press, 2015).

3. I didn't read it until the translation appeared later in *America* magazine. See Antonio Spadaro, SJ, "A big heart open to God: An interview with Pope Francis," *America*, September 30, 2013, https:// www.americamagazine.org/faith/2013/09/30/big-heart-open-god -interview-pope-francis.

4. In fact, during my term at the embassy, the Democratic Republic of Congo occupied an important portion of our work and reporting. Special envoys to the Great Lakes region in Africa, Russ Feingold and then Tom Perriello, were frequent visitors. We arranged what they felt were important meetings and contacts at various offices in the Vatican and with other organizations focused on Burundi, Rwanda, and the Democratic Republic of the Congo.

5. Pope Francis, "Address to the Members of the Diplomatic Corps Accredited to the Holy See," January 12, 2015, https://www.vatican.va/content/francesco/en/speeches/2015/january/documents/papa-francesco_20150112_corpo-diplomatico.html.

6. Mattathias Schwartz, "Letter from Lampedusa—the anchor," *The New Yorker*, April 14, 2021, https://www.newyorker.com/magazine/letter-from-lampedusa.

3. Meeting Pope Francis

1. You will read of the New York Federal Reserve Bank later.

2. Elisabetta Piqué, *Pope Francis: Life and Revolution* (Chicago: Loyola Press, 2013). I had known Elisabetta's husband, Gerry O'Connell, the Vatican correspondent for the Jesuit magazine *America*, for some time. He was a wonderful source of knowledge, but it was much later in my stay that I got to know Elisabetta.

3. Ernesto Cavassa, "On the Trail of Aparecida: Jorge Bergoglio and the Latin American Ecclesial Tradition," *America*, October 30, 2013.

4. "U.S. Spy Agency Denies that It Eavesdropped on Vatican," Reuters.com, October 30, 2013, https://www.reuters.com/article/vatican-usa-spying/u-s-spy-agency-denies-that-it-eavesdropped-on-vatican-idINDEE99T0BO20131030.

5. Pope Francis, *The Name of God Is Mercy: A Conversation with Andrea Tornielli* (New York: Random House, 2016).

6. Cf. Pope Francis, Angelus, March 17, 2013; see also Walter Kasper, *Mercy* (Mahwah, NJ: Paulist Press, 2013).

7. Susan Hayward and Katherine Marshall, eds., *Women, Religion, and Peacebuilding: Illuminating the Unseen* (Washington, DC: United States Institute of Peace, 2015), https://www.usip.org/publications/2015/09/women-religion-and-peacebuilding.

8. Hayward and Marshall, *Women, Religion, and Peacebuilding*, 42.

9. See Talitha Kum, https://www.talithakum.info.

10. Robin Gomes, "Pope: More Church Sectors Needed in Fight against Human Trafficking," *Vatican News*, September 26, 2019, https://www.vaticannews.va/en/pope/news/2019-09/pope-francis-talitha-kum-human-trafficking-commitment-church.html.

11. A synod is a council of a church, usually convened to decide an issue of doctrine, administration, or application. It is usually an assembly of the clergy and sometimes also the laity in a diocese or other division of the Church.

12. See "Iran Nuclear Deal: Key Details," BBC News, June 11, 2019, https://www.bbc.com.

4. A Challenge of the Conclave

1. Alessandro Bianchi, "Pope Fires Entire Board of Vatican Financial Watchdog," Reuters, June 5, 2014, https://www.reuters.com/article/us-vatican-pope-regulator/pope-fires-entire-board-of-vatican-financial-watchdog-idUSKBN0EG23F20140605.

2. Philip Pullella, "Exclusive: Vatican Inspectors Suspect Key Office Was Used for Money Laundering," Reuters, November 3, 2015, https://www.reuters.com/article/us-vatican-finances-apsa/exclusive-vatican-inspectors-suspect-key-office-was-used-for-money-laundering-idUSKCN0SS1RP20151103.

3. Vatican Information Service, "New Economic Framework for the Holy See," July 9, 2014, http://visnews-en.blogspot.com/2014/07/new-economic-framework-for-holy-see.html.

4. Philip Pullella, "Vatican's First Auditor-General Resigns Unexpectedly," Reuters, June 20, 2017, https://www.reuters.com/article/us-vatican-auditor/vaticans-first-auditor-general-resigns-unexpectedly-idUSKBN19B1YV.

5. Bambino Gesù Hospital falls under the oversight of the Secretariat of State. As the outgoing secretary of state, Cardinal Bertone was given an apartment in a building just next to Casa Santa Marta, which is a simple shared lodging where Pope Francis lives.

6. Jason Horowitz, "Two Ex-officials of Vatican-Run Hospital Charged with Misusing Money," *New York Times*, July 13, 2017,

https://www.nytimes.com/2017/07/13/world/europe/vatican
-cardinal-bertone-hospital.html.

7. Phillip Pullella, "Ex-head of Vatican Bank Sent to Trial on Embezzlement Charge," Reuters, March 2, 2018, https://www.reuters
.com/article/us-vatican-bank-trial/ex-head-of-vatican-bank-sent-to
-trial-on-embezzlement-charge-idUSKCN1GE2IF.

8. Inés San Martín, "Vatican Continues Its Financial Clean-up," *Crux*, April 27, 2018, https://cruxnow.com/vatican/2018/04/
vatican-continues-its-financial-clean-up.

9. Formerly known as the Financial Intelligence Authority (Italian: *Autorità di Informazione Finanziaria,* or AIF) is an institution connected to the Holy See and a canonical and Vatican civil juridic person established by Pope Benedict XVI on December 30, 2010. See https://www.aif.va.

10. See Council of Europe, https://www.coe.int.

11. "Italy Suspends Vatican Bank Card Payments," BBC
.com, January 3, 2013, https://www.bbc.com/news/world-europe
-20903443.

12. Davide Casati, "Of Virtue and Vice, and a Vatican Priest," *New York Times*, October 19, 2014, https://www.nytimes.com/2014/
10/19/business/of-virtue-and-vice-and-a-vatican-priest.html.

13. See Massimo Franco, "La rivincita della Curia nella finanza In bilico anche il presidente dello Ior," *Corriere della Sera,* July 28, 2017, https://www.corriere.it.

14. "Holy See Strengthens Anti-corruption Authority," *Vatican News*, February 9, 2019, https://www.vaticannews.va/en/vatican-city/
news/2019-02/holy-see-strengthens-anti-corruption-authority.html.

5. Diplomacy and Politics

1. Thomas Reese, "Vatican Questions Nuclear Deterrence," Berkley Center for Religion, Peace & World Affairs, May 12, 2010, https://berkleycenter.georgetown.edu/posts/vatican-questions
-nuclear-deterrence; Gerard O'Connell, "Nuclear Disarmament Now a 'Moral Imperative' as Pope Francis Rejects Deterrence," *America,*

November 13, 2017, https://www.americamagazine.org/politics
-society/2017/11/13/nuclear-disarmament-now-moral-imperative
-pope-francis-rejects.

2. ISIL (Islamic State of Iraq and the Levant) is synonymous
with ISIS.

3. John L. Allen Jr., "Why a Meeting between the Pope and
Russian Patriarch Is Finally Happening," *Crux*, February 5, 2016,
https://cruxnow.com/church/2016/02/05/why-a-meeting-between
-the-pope-and-russian-patriarch-is-finally-happening.

4. Bob Woodard and Scott Armstrong, *The Brethren* (New
York: Simon & Schuster, 1979).

5. "1999 Baltimore Orioles-Cuban National Team Exhibition Series," Baseball Reference, https://www.baseball-reference
.com/bullpen/1999_Baltimore_Orioles-Cuban_National
_Team_Exhibition_Series#:~:text=The%201999%20Baltimore
%20Orioles%20%2D%20Cuban,solely%20of%20major
%20league%20players.

6. Nicole Winfield, "Little-Known Book by Pope Outlines
Views, Hopes for Cuba," Associated Press, December 28, 2014, see
https://www.theday.com/article/20141228/ENT03/312289981.

7. Jon Lee Anderson, "A New Cuba," *The New Yorker,* September 26, 2016, https://www.newyorker.com/magazine/2016/10/
03/a-new-cuba.

6. Pope Francis Visits the United States

1. Paul Elie, *The Life You Save May Be Your Own: An American Pilgrimage* (New York: Farrar, Straus & Giroux, 2003).

2. David Brooks, *The Road to Character* (New York: Random
House, 2015).

3. Scott Pelley, "Pope Francis," *60 Minutes*, September 20,
2015, https://www.cbsnews.com/news/pope-francis-60-minutes
-scott-pelley/.

4. Pope Francis, "Transcript: Pope Francis's speech at the White House," *The Washington Post*, September 23, 2015, https://www.washingtonpost.com/local/social-issues/text-of-pope-franciss-speech-at-the-white-house/2015/09/23/27c70d74-61fb-11e5-9757-e49273f05f65_story.html.

7. The Pope at the Capitol

1. Interestingly, Speaker Boehner and three of his immediate predecessors and two successors are Catholic. Since 1962, there have been eleven speakers, eight of which have been Catholic.

2. Pope Francis, "Transcript: Pope Francis's speech to Congress," *The Washington Post*, September 24, 2015.

8. The New Chancery Building

1. Around 2005, the ambassador of the United States to Italy, Mel Sembler, convinced Congressman C. W. Bill Young (R-FL), chairman of the House Appropriations Committee, to appropriate $83 million for the purchase of a building that would be added to the campus of the U.S. Embassy in Italy and the UN Mission.

2. The U.S. Embassy to the Holy See is a part of the "Tri-mission Community" in Rome, the other two being the Embassy of the United States to Italy and the United States Mission to the UN Agencies in Rome.

3. A Leadership in Energy and Environmental Design (LEED) rating.

4. PolitiFact.Florida, "Fact Check: Jeb Bush Says Obama Closing Embassy to Vatican," *Record Eagle*, Traverse City, Florida, December 7, 2013, https://www.record-eagle.com/opinion/fact-check-jeb-bush-says-obama-closing-embassy-to-vatican/article_6214810c-d68b-5084-ade8-1e935b50ea2f.html.

9. The Making of an Encyclical

1. Pope Francis, apostolic exhortation *Evangelii Gaudium*, "The Joy of the Gospel," November 24, 2013, https://www.vatican.va/content/francesco/en/apost_exhortations/documents/papa-francesco_esortazione-ap_20131124_evangelii-gaudium.html. An apostolic exhortation is a magisterial document written by the pope. It is considered third in importance, after apostolic constitutions and encyclicals.

2. See Robert P. Imbelli, "The Principled Ambivalence of Pope Francis," *First Things*, November 7, 2017, https://www.firstthings.com/web-exclusives/2017/11/the-principled-ambivalence-of-pope-francis.

3. Pope Francis, "Pope Francis' Address to Diplomatic Corps," *Vatican News*, January 7, 2019, https://www.vaticannews.va/en/pope/news/2019-01/pope-francis-address-to-diplomatic-corps.html.

4. There was a 2006 documentary film directed by David Guggenheim about Vice President Gore's efforts to educate and move the U.S. public to act on global climate change. See Al Gore, "An Inconvenient Truth," Lawrence Bender Productions, May 24, 2006, https://www.imdb.com.

5. Pierre Teilhard de Chardin, *Hymn of the Universe* (New York: Harper & Row, 1961), https://www.religion-online.org/book/hymn-of-the-universe/.

6. Pope Francis, *Laudato Si'* (On Care of Our Common Home), May 24, 2015, https://www.vatican.va/content/francesco/en/encyclicals/documents/papa-francesco_20150524_enciclica-laudato-si.html. The Latin title is taken from the first phrase of a song or poem to the sun written by St. Francis of Assisi about God's creation. Roughly translated it means, "Praise be to Thee."

7. Since his election, Pope Francis has so far issued three encyclicals: *Lumen Fidei* (June 29, 2013), *Laudato Si'* (May 24, 2015), and *Fratelli Tutti* (October 3, 2020); and five apostolic exhortations: *Evangelii Gaudium* (November 24, 2013), *Amoris Laetitia* (March 19, 2016), *Gaudete et Exsultate* (March 19, 2018), *Christus Vivit* (March

25, 2019), and *Querida Amazonia* (February 2, 2020), see https://
www.vatican.va.

10. The Vatican

1. The Pontifical Council Cor Unum for Human and Christian Development was a dicastery of the Roman Curia of the Catholic Church from 1971 to 2016.

2. See "The Secretariat of State," https://www.vatican.va/
roman_curia/secretariat_state/index.htm.

3. Pope Francis, apostolic letter issued motu proprio, *Fidelis Dispensator et Prudens*, February 24, 2014, https://www.vatican.va/
content/francesco/en/motu_proprio/documents/papa-francesco
-motu-proprio_20140224_fidelis-dispensator-et-prudens.html.

4. It is also known by its former title, the Sacred Congregation for the Propagation of the Faith, or simply the *Propaganda Fide.*

5. Hannah Brockhaus, "Cardinal Tagle Named Head of Propaganda Fide, Vatican Evangelization Office," aciafrica.org, December 8, 2019, https://www.aciafrica.org/news/518/cardinal-tagle-named
-head-of-propaganda-fide-vatican-evangelization-office.

6. This third dicastery also has three commissions: the first on Charitable Work and Human Promotion (formerly Cor Unum); the second on Ecology (work that had been handled by the Pontifical Council for Justice and Peace); and a third one on Health (formerly the Pontifical Council on Health).

7. The Pontifical Council for Culture traces its origins to the Second Vatican Council and its desire to be open to that great, dynamic, multiform world of contemporary culture. See http://www
.cultura.va.

8. Pontifical Academy of Sciences, "Trafficking in Human Beings: Modern Slavery," Workshop, November 2–3, 2013, http://
www.pas.va.

9. Pontifical Academy of Sciences, "Young People against Prostitution and Human Trafficking: The Greatest Violence against

Women," Joint Workshop of the PAS and the Global Freedom Network, November 15–16, 2014, http://www.pas.va.

10. Oliver Milman, "Andrew Forrest Signs Up Religious Forces to Fight Slavery and Trafficking," *The Guardian*, March 17, 2014, https://www.theguardian.com/world/2014/mar/18/andrew-forrest -signs-up-religious-forces-to-fight-slavery-and-trafficking.

11. Interestingly, as if nobody in the State Department got the message that the Vatican is extremely cautious about being used for political purposes, in October 2020 the then secretary of state Mike Pompeo undertook a rapidly planned visit to the Vatican to meet the pope. The Vatican turned down the meeting, stating that it was too close to the presidential elections.

11. The Diplomatic Corps

1. See the Acton Institute, https://www.acton.org.

2. "2014–2016 Ebola Outbreak in West Africa," Centers for Disease Control and Prevention, page last reviewed March 8, 2019, https://www.cdc.gov/vhf/ebola/history/2014-2016-outbreak/.

3. See "Sierra Leone's Ebola Crisis in Pictures," Caritas Internationalis, November 10, 2014, https://www.caritas.org/2014/11/ sierra-leones-ebola-crisis-pictures/.

4. "'No Touch' Rules in Africa after Ebola," Caritas Internationalis, September 29, 2014, https://www.caritas.org/2014/09/no -touch-rules-in-africa-after-ebola/.

5. "A Discussion with Sister Barbara Brillant," Berkley Center for Religion, Peace, & World Affairs, December 10, 2016, https:// berkleycenter.georgetown.edu/interviews/a-discussion-with-sister -barbara-brillant.

6. Robert Vitillo, "A Roadmap for the Future of Children with HIV," Caritas.org, April 11, 2016, https://www.caritas.org/2016/04/a -roadmap-for-the-future-of-children-with-hiv/.

12. *Congedo*

1. "Armenian Assembly of America Reflects on Pope Francis' Trip to Armenia," *Aravot–Armenian News*, June 29, 2016, https://www.aravot-en.am/2016/06/29/178210/.

2. Joanna Berendt, "Pope Francis, Visiting Auschwitz, Asks God for the 'Grace to Cry,'" *New York Times*, July 30, 2016, https://www.nytimes.com/2016/07/30/world/europe/pope-francis-auschwitz.html.

3. Codels offer a great opportunity to explain issues and their significance to congressional leaders in an ambiance that is more relaxed and conducive to discussion than in their Washington offices. As such, significant staff time is dedicated to preparing and accompanying them to arranged meetings.

4. Domani Spero, "Foreign Service Tradition: Political Ambassadors Have to Be out by January 20," *Diplopundit*, January 6, 2017, https://diplopundit.net/tag/marc-grossman/.

5. Francis Rooney, *The Global Vatican: An Inside Look at the Catholic Church, World Politics, and the Extraordinary Relationship between the United States and the Holy See* (Lanham, MD: Rowman & Littlefield, 2013).

6. Pope Francis, postsynodal apostolic exhortation, *Amoris Laetitia*, March 19, 2016, https://www.vatican.va/content/dam/francesco/pdf/apost_exhortations/documents/papa-francesco_esortazione-ap_20160319_amoris-laetitia_en.pdf.

7. See also Pope Francis, *The Name of God Is Mercy* (New York: Random House, 2017).

8. The motto of Pope Francis is taken from a passage from the venerable Bede, homily 21 (CCL 122, 149–51), on the Feast of Matthew, which reads, *Vidit ergo Jesus publicanum, et quia miserando atque eligendo vidit, ait illi, "Sequere me"* [Jesus therefore sees the tax collector, and since he sees by having mercy and by choosing, he says to him, "Follow me"], https://www.vatican.va.

INDEX

*Page numbers in **bold** refer to images.*

the Financing of Terrorism (MONEYVAL), 54

Communism, 65–66

Community of Sant'Egidio, 69–70

Congedo, 157–58

Congregation for the Doctrine of the Faith, 120

Congregation for the Evangelization of Peoples, 121

Congregation for the Oriental Churches, 120–21

Congregations, 120–21

Congress, U.S., 92–94. *See also* Address to Congress, Francis

Coogan, Steve, 130–31

COP 21 (2015 United Nations Climate Change Conference), 111

Council for the Economy, 120

Councils, 122–23

Creagen, James, 107

Creation, 93

Cricket, 139

Crowley, Jim, 99

Cuba, xviii, xx, 65–71, 77, 79, 85

Culture of engagement, 45–46

Day, Dorothy, 93

de Chardin, Pierre Teilhard, 114

De Franssu, Jean-Baptiste, 58

de la Jara, Mónica Jiménez, 140

Democratic Republic of Congo, 23, 164n4

Department of State. *See* State Department

Department of Treasury and State, 53–56

Destinations, Francis's visit to America, 75

Diaz, Carlos, 56

Diaz, Miguel, 5, 16

Dicasteries, 121–22

Directorate for Security Services and Civil Protection, 81

Dirty war, Argentinean, 37

Dolan, Timothy, 98

Dominican Republic, 125

Donfried, Karen, xiii

Draper, Robert, 78

Dunford, Joseph, 156

Ebola, 28, 150, 152

Egan, Eileen, xx–xxi

Election of Francis, 7–8

Electors, cardinal, 160

Embassy, new, **89**, 103–9, 169n1

Encyclicals, 111–15

Eritrea, 26–27

Evangelii Gaudium, 111–12

Farrell, Kevin, 121

Fenway, 158

Ferragosto, 108

Fiat Cinque Cento, 80, 84–85, **88**

Filoni, Fernando, 121

Financial Intelligence Authority, 54, 58

Flanigan, Tim, 28, 151

Flynn, Ray, 18–19